Spirit Anew
SINGING PRAYER & PRAISE

Spirit Anew

SINGING PRAYER & PRAISE

Coordinating Editor
Alan C. Whitmore

WOOD LAKE BOOKS

Coordinating editor: Alan C. Whitmore
Editor: Dianne Greenslade
Editorial team: Andrew Dreitcer, Wayne Irwin, Eileen M. Johnson,
Stephen M. Lee, Flora Litt, Jeeva Sam, Gordon Walt, Heather Walt
Cover design and artwork: Margaret Kyle
Permissions: Lindy Jones
Interior design: Margaret Kyle and Julie Bachewich
Consulting art director: Robert MacDonald

We acknowledge the financial support of the Government of Canada through the
Book Publishing Industry Development Program for our publishing activities.

At WOOD LAKE BOOKS we practice what we publish, guided by
a concern for fairness, justice, and equal opportunity in all of
our relationships with employees and customers.

Wood Lake Books Inc. is committed to caring for the environment
and all creation. We recycle, reuse and compost, and encourage readers to do the same.
Resources are printed on recycled paper and more environmentally friendly groundwood papers
(newsprint), whenever possible. A portion of all profit is donated to charitable organizations.

Canadian Cataloguing in Publication Data
Main entry under title:
Spirit anew [music]
Editor Canadian.
Includes index.
ISBN 1-55145-345-2 (Pew ed.)
1. Sacred vocal music. I. Whitmore, Alan C.
M1999.S759 1999   782.2'2171   C99-910252-4

Published by
Wood Lake Books Inc.
Kelowna, British Columbia, Canada
e-mail: info@woodlake.com
1.250.766.2778
www.joinhands.com

Printing 9 8 7 6 5 4 3 2 1

Printed in Canada by
Transcontinental Printing

Spirit Anew *is dedicated*
to Diane Richard & The French Connection,
in gratitude for the hospitality and spirit
which nourished the editorial team.

Introduction

*F*ar too often worship is a "head" experience. The liturgy we use, the multi-stanza hymns we sing, and the prayers we hear prayed on our behalf can keep us from feeling the presence of God.

Spirit Anew is intended to help people make a heart connection within worship. The songs found in this book tend to be less wordy and easier to sing than standard worship music. These songs provide music that allows us to enter into a deeper experience of God. It is the music of prayer and praise.

Singing as Prayer

To quote Aldous Huxley, "After silence, that which comes nearest to express-ing the inexpressible is music." When we add word to music, we add that which makes us uniquely human among creatures. Thus we are enabled not only to come, in a measure, near to "expressing the inexpressible," but also enabled to express our innate longing for communion with the Holy Other-ness of our being.

It has been said that to sing is to pray twice. A prayer song is uniquely able to help us express the affections of the heart as well as the mind. Singing our prayer engages the whole being in a way that is indeed praying twice and more!

For centuries the Christian Church has found its favorite prayer in the psalm – the sung prayers. In our personal and communal prayer, we have chanted and sung them in metrical and paraphrased form down through the history of Christendom. Sometimes called "The Prayer Book of the Bible" the psalms have put words to our deepest love, longings, and laments; our suffering, doubts, and celebrations; our thanksgivings, praise, and petitions.

In prayer, we open ourselves to awareness of God's presence with us at all times and in all places in this and all dimensions of life. In prayer, we respond with our whole being to God's communication through Christ. To pray is to experience the relationship that is God's gift of love and grace to us and all people, and indeed to all creation. And to sing our prayer – whether of ado-ration, confession, thanksgiving, or petition – is to joint spirit, soul, and body in giving ourselves to this relationship.

Prayer is not only affirmation of faith and the Christian story. Prayer is being with God in the integrity of our real selves; addressing God, speaking directly to God, and listening to God.

Many of the hymns we have known and loved are prayers of direct address, and these have touched our hearts as well as our minds. Particularly if these were simple in word content, with repetition and a chorus, we easily committed them to memory and carried these sung prayers into our personal devotions in daily life. We sang those chorus-type songs with zest or in quiet meditation and often found ourselves lifted into heavenly places as we were able to let go of our focus upon the page in the hymnbook and let the prayer become our own. We were moved in our inner being; we were changed.

Today many new songs – songs written from the heart – give voice to our prayers. Some of these have arisen from overflowing gratitude for blessings; some, such as African-American spirituals, from the agony of oppression and persecution.

The songs in this collection will help us to offer authentic prayer – prayer from the heart and the head, prayer from the depths of faith, hope, and love. These prayers in song to God acknowledge our creatureliness, and our need with that of the whole creation for sustenance and the grace of the gospel. They include prayers of wonder and waiting, of risking and resting in God. This blend of word, music, and instrumentation uniquely unites body, soul, and spirit in the harmony of intent and desire that is prayer.

Naming God

"God is spirit," says John 4:24. Though we see the presence of God in the life of Jesus, we still grope for words to express something of who and what this mysterious Spirit is. Our ancestors in the faith similarly struggled to speak of God. The ancient Hebrew Scriptures refer to God with the holy Tetragrammaton, YHWH. The name of God – which was not to be spoken – may have meant something like "I am who I am" or "I will be who I will be." It suggests the depth of God's mystery and the endless, timeless expanse of God's being.

In recognition of the many ways the Divine Presence exceeds our understandings, the selections in this book contain a wide variety of scripturally based word-images, metaphors, and words for God. One of these words, LORD, is used as a substitute for the Hebrew word YHWH. Of course, LORD is not an accurate translation of YHWH, and its convention of usage comes out of particular cultural experiences of the relationship between a king and his subjects that may be foreign to us – and may carry negative connotations for some. In fact, no good contemporary substitute for YHWH has developed in the Christian community.

In *Spirit Anew*, we have chosen to use LORD sparingly and carefully, mindful as we are of the difficulties it presents, as well as the long and valued tradition of referring to God in this way. So, LORD appears when the book's editors or the song's writers firmly believed the piece would suffer poetically or theologically if the words were rewritten to eliminate it. Further, LORD appears as one among the many ways Christians have attempted to give expression to their experiences of a God whose nature we can never comprehend – even as this Divine Mystery invites us to clearer comprehension, to deeper intimacy.

Styles of Music

The selections in *Spirit Anew* vary widely in musical style. There are praise choruses, African-American spirituals, mantric chants and prayers, songs in litany style, canons/rounds and multi-stanza songs (in the style of a traditional hymn). Many of the selections appear in print for the first time in *Spirit Anew*.

Worship should be the best gift we give to our God. Therefore an explanation of how to "present" some of these musical styles follows. This will hopefully enable everyone to partake of the treasures that exist in this book.

African-American Spirituals

There are 17 African-American Spirituals (A-AS) in *Spirit Anew*. These spirituals have been arranged in the vocal/piano African-American gospel music style of Willie P. Dorsey, Sr., (1954-1997) and Stephen M. Lee. Any singer/musician who is acquainted with traditional practices in notating A-AS, will immediately recognize a departure from the norm in these arrangements.

1. In *Spirit Anew*, all of the A-AS are notated in compound time, i.e., 12/8. By contrast, the majority of A-AS in mainline denominational hymnals and hymnal supplements are notated in simple time, i.e., 2/4, 3/4, 4/4, 4/8.

    When A-AS are notated in compound time they are transformed from a strictly Western notational style and rhythmic feel to an "Africanized" notational style and rhythmic feel, i.e., in the style of the so-called "gospel waltz." This "Africanized" notational style and rhythmic feel will help the singer/musician to interpret the African-American Gospel (A-AG) music style of Willie P. Dorsey and Stephen M. Lee.

2. The tempos of the A-AS are given as suggested tempos only. Ultimately, the tempo of a song will depend upon the musical/technical ability of the singer/musician and upon the context in which the A-AS is being used. For example, the A-AS, "I Want Jesus to Walk with Me," could be sung at the suggested tempo where a slow meditative mood is desired, or a much faster tempo where a majestic or noble mood is desired.

3. All the A-AS are arranged in "flat" keys. These keys are popular among many A-AG keyboard musicians. The keys used comfortably situate the vocal line of these A-AS for congregational singing. Occasionally, a seemingly out of range note may appear within the vocal line, as in the song "I'm Gonna Live So God Can Use Me." This note, however, is only a suggested alternate note which is sung in some African-American churches by a skilled soprano in order to add color and drama.

4. Embellishment of the vocal melody by the right-hand piano line may occur during measures where the vocal line is stationary, i.e., where the vocal line either rests or sustains a note. This piano embellishment serves to fill in the empty spaces, so to speak, but more importantly, illustrates the relationship between vocal and piano line in A-AG music. The piano is not the accompaniment, but instead, it is the complement.

5. Nine of the A-AS make use of nonstandard English or African-American folk vernacular, i.e., deliberate omissions in word pronunciations, spelling, and grammatical usage. This selective use of the folk vernacular is rooted in praxis. These are the A-AS heard and experienced in the folk vernacular tradition. The other A-AS have been heard and experienced in the standard English tradition. In deciding whether or not to borrow from the folk vernacular tradition, the singer/musician must use her/his musical instinct, i.e., what feels most natural to the tongue, to the ear, and to the heart.

Finally, the singer/musician should never become a slave to the printed notes, for A-AG music is rooted in improvisation. It is hoped that the performer of these A-AS will feel free to add to or take away from these arrangements as needed. These are not the definitive source nor summit of the A-AG music style. These arrangements are intended to offer the singer/musician a glimpse into what some African-Americans have seen, heard, and experienced in African-American worship.

Mantric Chants

The repetitive, mantra-like chants in *Spirit Anew* rise out of an ancient Christian prayer form called *lectio divina,* or "divine reading." This type of prayer emphasizes a stance of open receptivity before God. In part, this openness is deepened by the repeating of spiritual texts. These texts may be passages of scripture, reflections on wonders of God's creation, or ruminations on life with God.

Mantric chants set such texts to music. Instead of giving us quantities of information about God, these chants provide a musical opening to God's presence, a context for an intimate encounter with God. First and foremost these chants are prayers – prayers that turn us toward God. They invite us to linger with God, resting, carried for a time in divine arms, lost in the wonder of the Holy Presence.

In their simplicity, the songs invite us to "pray without ceasing," to sing them again and again until their biblical words and images permeate our being. As we enter into the music, we may begin to discover new meaningfulness in our lives with God. In addition, the music may draw us to a time of simply resting with God, silently enjoying the presence of God as we are carried by the music around us. At some point the chants may become the prayers by which we express ourselves to God, prayers that bubble up within us throughout our days.

Use of Instruments

The human voice is the principal musical instrument in prayer and praise. All other instruments are there to assist.

There are a variety of ways to present the songs found in *Spirit Anew.* The first is voices alone, or a cappella. Most canons/rounds in this book are printed without instrumental accompaniment. There are also some unaccompanied mantras/chants. These songs become their perfect gift when only the human voice is heard.

The organ, historically the principal accompanying instrument, is also used in *Spirit Anew.* However, it by no means holds its traditional predominance. Use the organ with care. Accompaniments should be supportive and complementary, nor overpowering.

The piano has an important part to play. Not only are there songs which are specifically pianistic, but everything which might be played on the organ, can also be played very successfully on the piano. In most cases, be careful not to overpedal. Keep the sonorities clean and supportive.

In recent years, the guitar has increasingly become an instrument of choice. Numerous songs in *Spirit Anew* can be accompanied by guitar. There are even some where it is preferable. Guitar chords have been provided for those songs where guitar is appropriate. The African-American spiritual arrangements are very pianistic. Therefore, guitar chords in capo position only are found in the Pew edition for those occasions when guitar is the only instrument available, or the instrument of choice.

Much of the music in *Spirit Anew* is improvisational in nature. This also applies to adding other melodic instruments. Some obligati have been provided in the Music Leader's edition, however players are encouraged to be creative and add musicians as they are available.

If the 1970s and 1980s were the decades of the guitar, the 1990s and onward may be the time of the drum and other percussion. An increased interest in music from other cultures has spawned an awareness of the beauty and appropriateness of good drumming. Much of the music in *Spirit Anew* is suited to the addition of percussion. Be creative and adventurous in your music making.

Spirit Anew: Singing Prayer & Praise is an exciting music resource. Sing from your heart. Sing your prayer. Sing your praise. Most importantly, sing as your gift to God – the Creator, the Redeemer, and the Spirit.

May God richly bless your worship and your life.
The Editorial Team
    Andrew Dreitcer
    Wayne Irwin
    Eileen M. Johnson
    Stephen M. Lee
    Flora Litt
    Jeeva Sam
    Gordon Walt
    Heather Walt
    Alan C. Whitmore, Team Facilitator

A Child of God

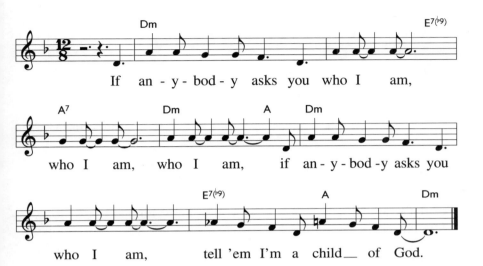

If an-y-bod-y asks you who I am,

who I am, who I am, if an-y-bod-y asks you

who I am, tell 'em I'm a child of God.

Words: African–American spiritual
Music: African–American spiritual
Arrangement in the African-American gospel music style of Willie P. Dorsey, Sr.
Arrangement copyright © 1998 Professional Music Services, Inc., New Orleans, LA. All rights reserved. Used by permission.

A Touching Place

Tune: Dream Angus (Scottish Traditional)

Christ's   is   the   world   in   which   we   move,
Feel   for   the   peo - ple   we   most   a - void,
Feel   for   the   par - ents   who've   lost   their   child,
Feel   for   the   lives   by   life   con - fused,

Christ's   are   the   folk   we're   sum - moned   to   love,
Strange   or   be - reaved   or   nev - er   em - ployed;
Feel   for   the   wom - en   whom   men   have   de - filed,
Rid - dled   with   doubt,   in   lov - ing   a - bused;

Christ's   is   the   voice   which   calls   us   to   care,   And
Feel   for   the   wom - en,   and   feel   for   the   men   Who
Feel   for   the   ba - by   for   whom   there's   no   breast,   And
Feel   for   the   lone - ly   heart,   con - scious   of   sin,   Which

Christ   is   the   one   who   meets   us   here.
fear   that   their   liv - ing   is   all   in   vain.
feel   for   the   wear - y   who   find   no   rest.
longs   to   be   pure   but   fears   to   be - gin.

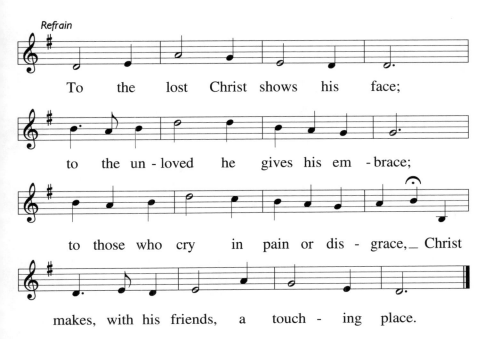

Refrain

To the lost Christ shows his face;

to the un-loved he gives his em-brace;

to those who cry in pain or dis-grace,__ Christ

makes, with his friends, a touch-ing place.

Words: The Iona Community
Music: traditional
Arrangement: The Iona Community
Words and arrangement copyright © 1989 WGRG The Iona Community (Scotland).
Used by permission of GIA Publications, Inc.

Alleluia, Sing!

Bless - ed be our__ God! Bless - ed be our__
Gift of love and__ peace! Gift of love and__
Come, O Spir - it of truth! Come, O Spir - it of

God! Joy of our hearts, source of all life and
peace! Je - sus the Christ, Je - sus our hope and
truth! Prom - ise of hope, kind - ness and mer -

love! God of heav - en and earth!
light! A flame of faith in our hearts! A
cy! Come and dwell in our hearts!

God of heav - en and earth!
flame of faith in our hearts! Pro -
Come and dwell in our hearts!

Words: David Haas
Music: David Haas
Words and music copyright © 1968 GIA Publications, Inc.

4

Alive! Alive!

A - live, a - live, a - live for - ev - er - more; Christ

Je - sus is a - live, a - live for - ev - er - more.   A -

live, a - live, a - live for - ev - er - more; Christ

Je - sus is a - live.   Sing hal - le -

lu - jah, sing hal - le - lu - jah; Christ Je - sus is a -

live for - ev - er - more. Sing hal - le - lu - jah, sing hal - le -

lu - jah; Christ Je - sus is a - live.

Words: Unknown   *Music:* Unknown
Arrangement: John T. Benson Publishing Company

By the Waters of Babylon

5

Tune: By the Waters

By	the	wa - ters,	the wa - ters	of
On	the	wil - lows,	the wil - lows	of
Those	who	car - ried us,	who car - ried us	to
On	the	al - ien soil,	the al - ien soil	of
By	the	wa - ters,	the wa - ters	of

Bab - y - lon,	we	sat down and	wept,	and
Bab - y - lon,	we	hung up our	harps,	our
Bab - y - lon,	asked	us for a	song,	a
Bab - y - lon,	how	dare we to	praise,	to
Bab - y - lon,	we	sat down and	wept,	and

wept	for	thee, Zi - on.	
harps	brought	from Zi - on.	
song	of	thee, Zi - on.	We re - mem - ber
praise	thy	God, Zi - on.	
wept	for	thee, Zi - on.	

thee, re - mem - ber thee, re - mem - ber thee, Zi - on.

Words: Carl P. Daw, Jr.
Music: traditional

6

Bread Is Broken

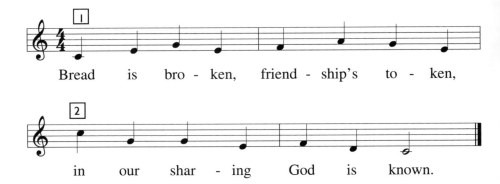

Bread is bro - ken, friend - ship's to - ken,

in our shar - ing God is known.

Words: Diane Taylor and Ken Powers
Music: Diane Taylor and Ken Powers
Words and music copyright © 1991 Prairie Rose Publications.

7

Christ Is Born

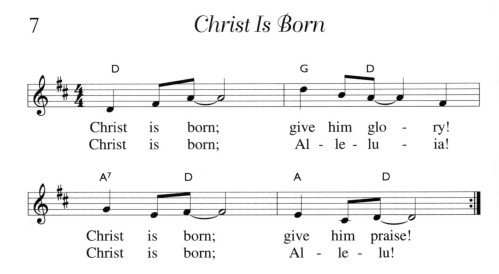

Christ is born; give him glo - ry!
Christ is born; Al - le - lu - ia!

Christ is born; give him praise!
Christ is born; Al - le - lu!

Words: traditional Byzantine Christmas prayer
Music: Raquel Mora Martinez
Music copyright © 1992 Abingdon Press. (Administered by The Copyright Company, Nashville, TN.)
All rights reserved. International copyright secured. Used by permission.

Christ Is Risen from the Dead

Tune: King of Kings

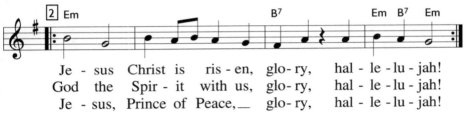

Easter Christ is ris-en from the dead,— glo-ry, hal-le-lu-jah!
Pentecost God the Spir-it dwells with-in us, glo-ry, hal-le-lu-jah!
Reign of King of kings and Lord of lords— glo-ry, hal-le-lu-jah!
Christ

Je - sus Christ is ris-en, glo-ry, hal - le -lu - jah!
God the Spir-it with us, glo-ry, hal - le -lu - jah!
Je - sus, Prince of Peace,— glo-ry, hal - le -lu - jah!

Words: anonymous
Music: Hasidic folk melody

9   *Change My Heart, Oh God*

Words: based on Psalm 51:10, Eddie Espinosa
Music: Eddie Espinosa

Christmas Gloria

Glo - ri - a! Glo - ri - a in ex - cel - sis De - o.

Glo - ri - a! Glo - ri - a in ex - cel - sis De - o. De - o.

Words: traditional
Music: Kevin R. Hackett

Come! Come! Everybody Worship

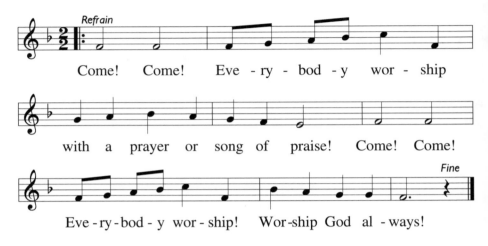

Come! Come! Eve - ry - bod - y wor - ship

with a prayer or song of praise! Come! Come!

Eve - ry - bod - y wor - ship! Wor-ship God al - ways!

Wor - ship and re - mem - ber to keep the Sab - bath day.
Wor - ship and re - mem - ber the Lord's un - end - ing care,
Wor - ship and re - mem - ber your bless - ings great and small.
Wor - ship and re - mem - ber how Je - sus long a - go
Wor - ship and re - mem - ber that God is like a light,

Take a rest and think of God; put your work a - way!
reach-ing out to love and help peo - ple eve - ry - where!
Give to God an of - fer - ing; show your thanks for all!
taught us how to talk to God; some-thing we should know!
show-ing you the way to go; ev - er burn - ing bright!

Words: Natalie Sleeth
Music: Natalie Sleeth

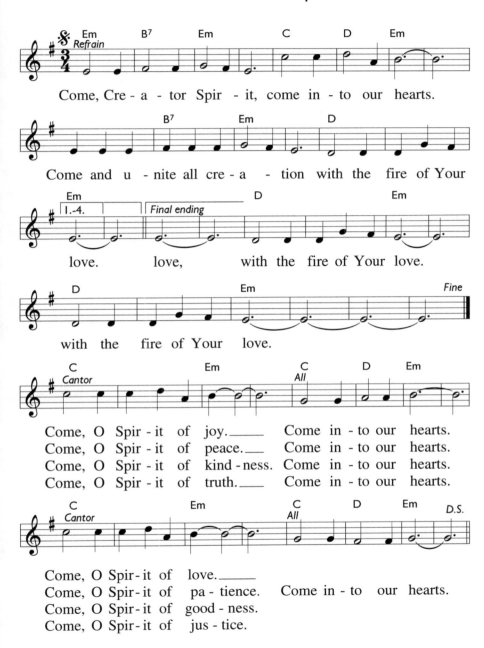

Come, Cre - a - tor Spir - it, come in - to our hearts.

Come and u - nite all cre - a - tion with the fire of Your

love. love, with the fire of Your love.

with the fire of Your love.

Come, O Spir - it of joy._____ Come in - to our hearts.
Come, O Spir - it of peace.___ Come in - to our hearts.
Come, O Spir - it of kind - ness. Come in - to our hearts.
Come, O Spir - it of truth.___ Come in - to our hearts.

Come, O Spir - it of love._____
Come, O Spir - it of pa - tience. Come in - to our hearts.
Come, O Spir - it of good - ness.
Come, O Spir - it of jus - tice.

Words: Weston Priory & Mary David Callahan, OSB
Music: Weston Priory & Mary David Callahan, OSB
Copyright 1990, 1994, from the recording *Song in our Silence*, The Benedictine Foundation of the State of Vermont, Inc.
Weston Priory, Weston, Vermont, USA. This arrangement by the Monks of Weston Priory and Sister Mary David Callahan, OSB.

Come, Lord Jesus

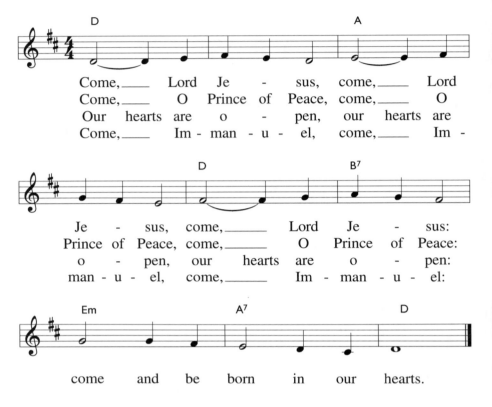

Come,___ Lord Je - sus, come,___ Lord
Come,___ O Prince of Peace, come,___ O
Our hearts are o - pen, our hearts are
Come,___ Im - man - u - el, come,___ Im -

Je - sus, come,___ Lord Je - sus:
Prince of Peace, come,___ O Prince of Peace:
o - pen, our hearts are o - pen:
man - u - el, come,___ Im - man - u - el:

come and be born in our hearts.

Words: Carey Landry
Music: Carey Landry

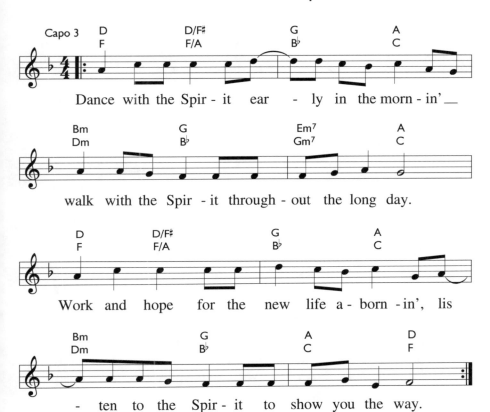

Words: Jim Strathdee
Music: Jim Strathdee
Words and music copyright © 1995 by Desert Flower Music, Carmichael, CA.

15

Come to My Heart

Come to my heart, Lord Je - sus;
Fill me with love, Lord Je - sus;
An - swer my pray'r, Lord Je - sus,

Teach me to walk in your way. Come to my heart, Lord
Teach me to walk in your way. Fill me with love, Lord
Teach me to walk in your way. An - swer my pray'r, Lord

Je - sus; Come to my heart to - day.
Je - sus; Fill me with love to - day.
Je - sus; An - swer my pray'r to - day.

Give me the peace and joy that on - ly you can bring.
Give me the peace and joy that on - ly you can bring.
Give me the peace and joy that on - ly you can bring.

Come to my heart, Lord Je - sus; Give me a song to sing.
Fill me with love, Lord Je - sus; Give me a song to sing.
An - swer my pray'r, Lord Je - sus; Give me a song to sing.

Words: Joe Pinson
Music: Joe Pinson
Words and music copyright © 1981 Joe Pinson. Used with permission.

(wide) Draw the cir-cle wide.   Draw it wid-er still.

Let this be our song, no one stands a-lone, stand-ing side by

side,   draw the cir - cle   wide.

Go back to the beginning last time   *Fine*

God the still - point of the cir - cle,
Let our hearts touch far hor - i - zons,
Let the dreams we dream be larg - er,

'Round whom all cre - a - tion turns;   No-thing lost, but
So en - com-pass great and small;   Let our lov-ing
Than we've ev - er dreamed be - fore;   Let the dream of

D.C. al Fine

held for - ev - er, in God's grac-ious arms.
know no bor - ders, Faith - ful to God's call.
Christ be in us, O - pen ev - ery door.

Words: Gordon Light
Music: Gordon Light
Words and music copyright © 1994 Common Cup Company.

17 Eat This Bread and Never Hunger

Tune: Modesto

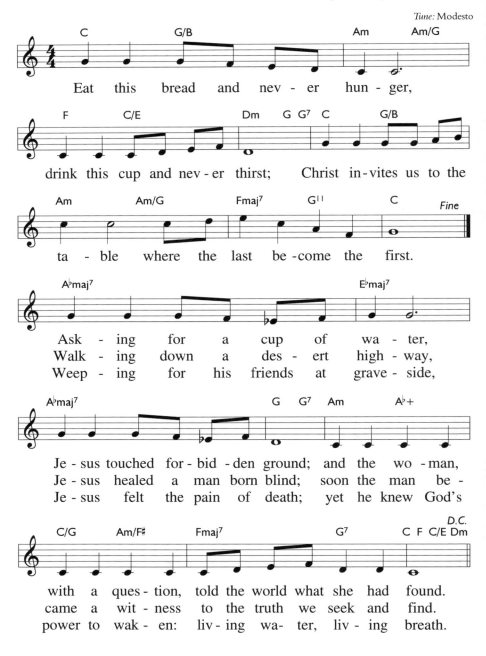

Words: Daniel Charles Damon
Music: Daniel Charles Damon

Glory, Glory Hallelujah

18

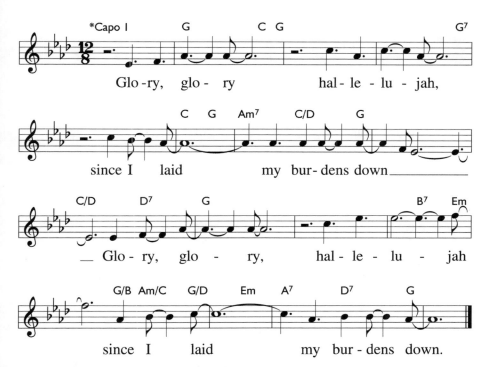

*The chords are for the use of guitarists only.

2. I feel better, so much better, since I laid...
3. Friends don't treat me like they used to, since I laid...

Words: African–American spiritual
Music: African–American spiritual
Arrangement in the African-American gospel music style of Willie P. Dorsey, Sr.
Arrangement copyright © 1998 Professional Music Services, Inc., New Orleans, LA. All rights reserved. Used by permission.

God of Love

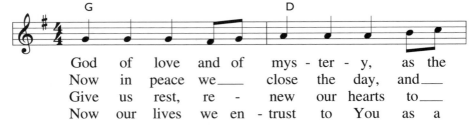

G   D

God of love and of mys - ter - y, as the
Now in peace we___ close the day, and___
Give us rest, re - new our hearts to___
Now our lives we en - trust to You as a

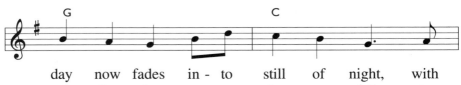

G   C

day now fades in - to still of night, with
ask for - give - ness___ when we fail to
rise a - gain with the dawn of day, to
song of praise, Gi - ver of the night. Up -

G   D

sim - ple hearts, filled with grat - i - tude, we give
give our - selves in the spir - it of Your___
work for peace and let jus - tice reign, giv - ing
hold us with Your___ Breath of love, the___

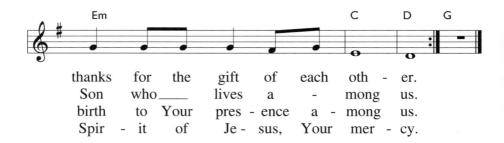

Em   C   D   G

thanks for the gift of each oth - er.
Son who___ lives a - mong us.
birth to Your pres - ence a - mong us.
Spir - it of Je - sus, Your mer - cy.

Words: Weston Priory & Mary David Callahan
Music: Weston Priory & Mary David Callahan
Copyright 1990, 1994, from the recording *Song in our Silence*, The Benedictine Foundation of the State of Vermont, Inc.
Weston Priory, Weston, Vermont, USA. This arrangement by the Monks of Weston Priory and Sister Mary David Callahan, OSB.

Words: Roger Jones
Music: Roger Jones
Words and music copyright © 1991 Christian Music Ministries, admin. by Sovereign Music UK, Leighton Buzzard Beds, UK.

God Please Forgive

We turn a - way from you, O God, each
Christ Je - sus came from you, O God, to

time we choose to do what's wrong; we're
help us know the way to live, to

sor - ry for the hurt we cause; God,
show us just how much you care, and

please for - give, and make us strong.
that you al - ways do for - give.

Words: Flora & Wayne
Music: Flora & Wayne
Words and music copyright © 1992, 1998 Flora Litt & Wayne Irwin.

God, you call us here to-geth-er, young and old, from near and far; we have come be-cause we love you, bring us close in mind and heart.

Words: Flora & Wayne
Music: Flora & Wayne
Words and music copyright © 1992, 1998 Flora Litt & Wayne Irwin.

23

Here I Stand

Here I stand be - fore your throne,
All I bring, I'm lay - ing down,

rea - dy, wait - ing, Yours a - lone.
nev - er - more to call my own.

Eve - ry - thing I lay at your feet;
Yours com - plete - ly, here I am;

Je - sus You are all that I could ev - er need.
lov - ing You, O Lord, be - fore your throne I stand.

Words: Ruth Fazal
Music: Ruth Fazal

He Is Our Peace

He is our peace who has bro - ken down ev - 'ry wall, He is our peace, He is our peace. He is our peace. Cast all your cares on Him, for He cares_ for you, He is our peace, He is our peace. Cast all your peace.

Words: Kandela Groves
Music: Kandela Groves

I Have Decided to Follow Jesus

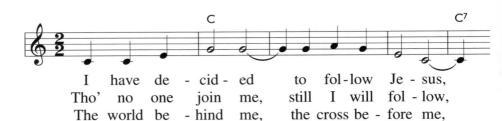

I have de - cid - ed to fol-low Je - sus,
Tho' no one join me, still I will fol - low,
The world be - hind me, the cross be - fore me,

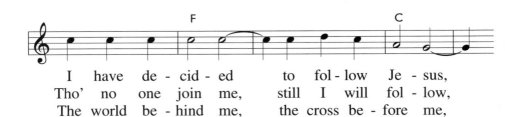

I have de - cid - ed to fol-low Je - sus,
Tho' no one join me, still I will fol - low,
The world be - hind me, the cross be - fore me,

I have de - cid - ed to fol-low Je - sus
Tho' no one join me, still I will fol - low
The world be - hind me, the cross be - fore me

No turn - ing back, no turn - ing back!

Words: Ascribed to an Indian prince
Music: Indian Folk melody, Paul B. Smith
Harmonization: N. Johnson

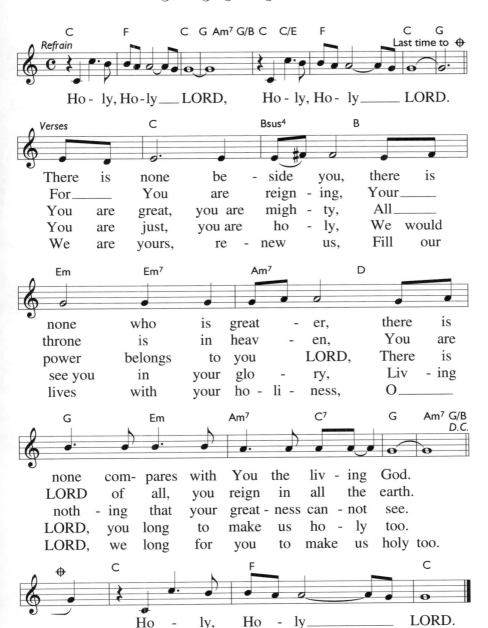

Refrain

Ho - ly, Ho-ly ___ LORD, Ho - ly, Ho - ly ___ LORD.

Verses

There is none be - side you, there is
For ___ You are reign - ing, Your ___
You are great, you are migh - ty, All ___
You are just, you are ho - ly, We would
We are yours, re - new us, Fill our

none who is great - er, there is
throne is in heav - en, You are
power belongs to you LORD, There is
see you in your glo - ry, Liv - ing
lives with your ho - li - ness, O ___

none com- pares with You the liv - ing God.
LORD of all, you reign in all the earth.
noth - ing that your great - ness can - not see.
LORD, you long to make us ho - ly too.
LORD, we long for you to make us holy too.

Ho - ly, Ho - ly ___ LORD.

Words: Ruth Fazal
Music: Ruth Fazal
Words and music copyright © 1993 Ruth Fazal. All rights reserved. International copyright secured.

27

Holy Light

Holy light, still burn - ing bright,
Holy fire, our heart's de - sire,
Holy word, all who have heard
Holy bread, our souls are fed,

pre - sence of God that frees_____ us.
dance of our life, pur - sue_____ us.
Je - sus walk - ing be - side_____ us.
cup_____ of love in - vite_____ us.

Lift_____ the shad - ows from_____ our soul,
Mend_____ our fro - zen bro - ken hearts,
Did not our hearts then burn_____ with love?
All_____ are wel - come at_____ the feast,

Shine through our life, Lord Je - sus.
Spir - it of God, re - new us.
Word of our God, now guide us.
Bread of the world u - nite us.

Words: Jim Strathdee
Music: Jim Strathdee
Words and music copyright © 1996 by Desert Flower Music, Carmichael, CA.

Hush

Hush, hush, some - bo - dy's call - in' mah name.

Hush, hush, some - bo - dy's call - in' mah name.____

Hush, hush, some - bo - dy's call - in' mah name.

Oh mah Lawd, oh mah Lawd, what shall I

do? what shall I do? do?

* The chords are for the use of guitarists only.

2. Sounds like Jesus, somebody's callin' mah name...
3. I'm so glad, trouble don't last always...

Words: African–American spiritual
Music: African–American spiritual
Arrangement in the African-American gospel music style of Willie P. Dorsey, Sr.
Arrangement copyright © 1998 Professional Music Services, Inc., New Orleans, LA. All rights reserved. Used by permission.

I Am the Resurrection

Refrain

I am the res-ur-rec-tion and the life; All who be-lieve in me will nev-er__ die. I am the res-ur-rec-tion and the life; All who be-lieve in me will

1.-3. live a new life. *to verses* *4.* live, will live a new life.

Verses

I have come to bring__ the__ truth;
In my word_____ all will come to know
Keep in mind the things that I have said;

I have come__ to bring__ you__ life;
it is love__ which makes the spir-it grow;
re-mem-ber me in the break-ing of the bread;

to refrain
if you be-lieve, then you shall__ live.

Words: Ray Repp
Music: Ray Repp
Words and music copyright © 1967 by K & R Music, Inc., Churchville, MD. Used by permission.

I Want Jesus to Walk with Me

*The chords are for the use of guitarists only.

2. In my trials, Lord, walk with me...
3. Walk with me, Lord, walk with me...

Words: African–American spiritual
Music: African–American spiritual
Arrangement: Stephen M. Lee

I will sing, I will sing a song un - to the LORD. I will
Chorus: Al-le - lu, al - le - lu - ia glo - ry to the LORD. Al - le-

sing, I will sing a song un - to the LORD. I will
lu, al - le - lu - ia glo - ry to the LORD. Al - le-

sing, I will sing a song un - to the LORD. Al - le -
lu, al - le - lu - ia glo - ry to the LORD.

lu - ia, glo - ry to the LORD.

The chorus may be sung after each verse or as a concluding verse at the end.

This is a "zipper song." Please add your own verses where applicable. Some suggestions are:
We will laugh, we will laugh with God's joy in our hearts...
We will hope, we will hope for God's peace on the earth...
We will tell, we will tell good news about God's love...
We will dance, we will dance with joy and liberty...

Words: Max Dyer
Music: Max Dyer
Words and music copyright © 1974 Celebration. (Administered by The Copyright Company, Nashville, TN.)
All rights reserved. International copyright secured. Used by permission.

I Want to Praise Your Name

Praise with the trum - pet, Praise with the harp,
Moun - tains and val - leys, Riv - ers and seas,
Moth - ers and fath - ers, Daugh - ters and sons,

Praise with the tim - brel, the dance and the lyre;
Stars in the heav - ens and fish in the deep;
All of God's peo - ple, the old and the young;

Let ev - 'ry - thing that has breath give praise to God.
Let all cre - a - tion give praise to God on high.
Let all who hun - ger to do God's will give praise.

I want to praise your name.

I want to sing your good - ness. Glo - ry, O

God; Glo - ry. Glo

- ry.

Words: Psalm 148–150, adapted by Bob Hurd
Music: Bob Hurd

33   *I Will Trust in the Lord*

*The chords are for the use of guitarists only.

Words: African-American spiritual
Music: African-American spiritual
Arrangement in the African-American gospel music style of Willie P. Dorsey, Sr.
Arrangement copyright © 1998 Professional Music Services, Inc., New Orleans, LA.
All rights reserved. Used by permission.

I'm Gonna Live So

34

I'm gon - na live so God can use me an - y - time an - y - where____

I'm gon-na live so God can use me____ an - y - time an - y - where.

*The chords are for the use of guitarists only.

For additional verses use:
pray, love, serve, sing, shout, work, etc.

Words: African–American spiritual
Music: African–American spiritual
Arrangement in the African-American gospel music style of Willie P. Dorsey, Sr.
Arrangement copyright © 1998 Professional Music Services, Inc., New Orleans, LA.
All rights reserved. Used by permission.

If I Take the Wings

Tune: Clark

If I take the wings of the morn - ing and_
fly to the ends of the earth, I'll a - wake with the
dawn - ing to find_ you still_____ still with me.

Where shall I go from your Spir - it?
If I use night for my cov - er,
Dear God, you know all a - bout me;

How can I run from you? If I as -
will I then be a - lone? If I say,
know when I rise and fall. You know my

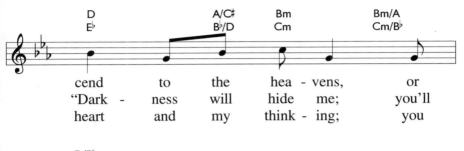

| D | | A/C# | Bm | | Bm/A |
| E♭ | | B♭/D | Cm | | Cm/B♭ |

cend   to   the   hea - vens,   or
"Dark - ness   will   hide me;   you'll
heart   and   my   think - ing;   you

| D/F# | | | |
| F/A | | | |

make   my   bed   in   hell,   you   are
nev - er   find   me   here,"   I   will
know   the   ways   I   try.   Be   my

| G(add2) | | | D/F# | | Em7 | Asus4 | |
| A♭(add2) | | | E♭/G | | Fm7 | B♭sus4 | D.C. |

there,   you   are   there   as   well.
find   you   are   al - ways   near.
guide   if   I   live   or   die.

Words: Daniel Charles Damon
Music: Daniel Charles Damon

I'm So Glad

*The chords are for the use of guitarists only.

2. Satan had me bound, but Jesus lifted me...
3. When I was in trouble Jesus lifted me...

Words: African–American spiritual
Music: African–American spiritual
Arrangement in the African-American gospel music style of Willie P. Dorsey, Sr.
Arrangement copyright © 1998 Professional Music Services, Inc., New Orleans, LA. All rights reserved. Used by permission.

*The chords are for the use of guitarists only.

2. Jesus already told me, ev'rything's...
3. The Holy Ghost done confirmed it, ev'rything's...

Words: African–American spiritual
Music: African–American spiritual
Arrangement in the African-American gospel music style of Willie P. Dorsey, Sr.
Arrangement copyright © 1998 Professional Music Services, Inc., New Orleans, LA. All rights reserved. Used by permission.

Jesus Be Praised

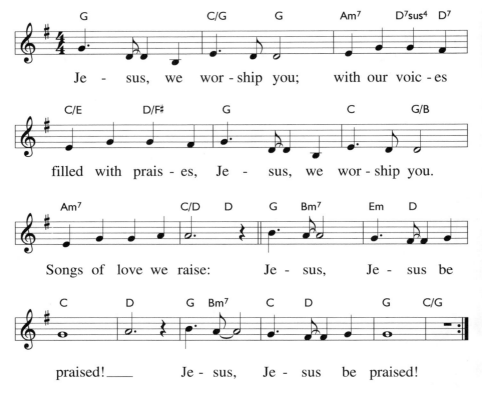

Je - sus, we wor - ship you; with our voic - es

filled with prais - es, Je - sus, we wor - ship you.

Songs of love we raise: Je - sus, Je - sus be

praised!____ Je - sus, Je - sus be praised!

Words: Handt Hanson
Music: Handt Hanson
Piano adaptation: Henry Wiens
Copyright © 1996 Changing Church, Inc.
Used with permission of Changing Church Forum/Prince of Peace Publishing.

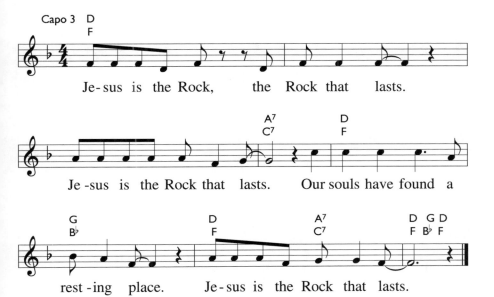

Capo 3 D / F

Je-sus is the Rock, the Rock that lasts.

A⁷ / C⁷   D / F

Je-sus is the Rock that lasts. Our souls have found a

G / B♭   D / F   A⁷ / C⁷   D G D / F B♭ F

rest-ing place. Je-sus is the Rock that lasts.

Individual names may be used in this song:
"(Name) is on the Rock...
(Her/his) soul has found a resting place...'

Words: Ghanian folk song
Music: Ghanian folk song
Arrangement: Betty Carr Pulkingham

Jesus, Name above All Names

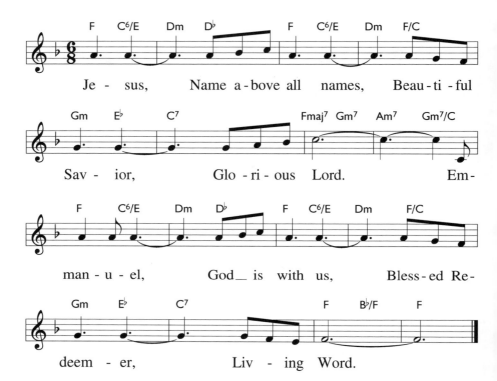

Je - sus, Name a - bove all names, Beau - ti - ful

Sav - ior, Glo - ri - ous Lord. Em -

man - u - el, God __ is with us, Bless - ed Re -

deem - er, Liv - ing Word.

Words: Naida Hearn
Music: Naida Hearn

Je-sus on the main-line tell 'im what cha want

Je-sus on the main-line tell 'im what cha want

Je-sus on the main-line tell 'im what cha want

Call 'im up and tell 'im what cha want.

*The chords are for the use of guitarists only.

2. If you're sick and you can't get well...
3. Call 'im up. Call 'im up...

Words: African–American spiritual
Music: African–American spiritual
Arrangement in the African-American gospel music style of Willie P. Dorsey, Sr.
Arrangement copyright © 1998 Professional Music Services, Inc., New Orleans, LA.
All rights reserved. Used by permission.

In My Name

Je -sus, you have called dis - ci - ples to your side;
Je -sus, you still call dis - ci - ples to your side;
Je -sus, help us bring the need - y to your side;

then you've sent them out to serve you far and wide;
then you send us out to serve you far and wide.
help us faith - ful - ly to serve you far and wide.

"Teach and preach and heal," you said, "let the hun - gry ones be fed,

and the lone- ly com - fort -ed in my name." in my name."

Words: Flora & Wayne
Music: Flora & Wayne
Words and music copyright © 1992 Flora Litt & Wayne Irwin.

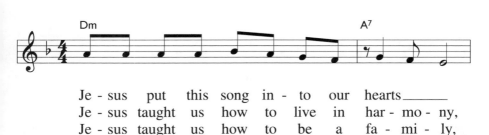

Je - sus put this song in - to our hearts_____
Je - sus taught us how to live in har - mo - ny,
Je - sus taught us how to be a fa - mi - ly,
Je - sus turned our sor - row in - to danc - ing,

Je - sus put this song in - to our hearts_____
Je - sus taught us how to live in har - mo - ny;
Je - sus taught us how to be a fa - mi - ly;
Je - sus turned our sor - row in - to danc - ing,

it's a song of joy no one can take___ a - way.___
dif- ferent fa - ces, dif- ferent ra - ces, he made us one.___
lov- ing one a - no - ther with the love that he gives.__
changed our tears of sad- ness in - to ri - vers of joy.___

Je - sus put this song_____ in - to our hearts.
Je - sus taught us how to live_____ in har - mo- ny.
Je - sus taught us how to be_____ a fa - mi- ly.
Je - sus turned our sor - rows_____ in- to a dance.

Words: Graham Kendrick
Music: Graham Kendrick
Words and music copyright © 1986 Thankyou Music. Administered by EMI Christian Music Publishing.

Jesus, Oh What a Wonderful Child

*The chords are for the use of guitarists only.

Words: African-American spiritual
Music: African-American spiritual
Arrangement in the African-American gospel music style of Willie P. Dorsey, Sr.

To create additional stanzas
Replace "life" with heart, mind, home, etc.

Words: Bob Kilpatrick
Music: Bob Kilpatrick
Words and music copyright © 1978 Bob Kilpatrick Music.
All rights reserved. International copyright secured. Assigned to The Lorenz Corporation 1998.

46   *Living in the Light*

Tune: Living in the Light

A light is gleam - ing,   spread - ing its

arms through- out the night,   liv - ing in the light.

Come share its glad - ness,   God's ra - diant

love is burn - ing bright,   liv -ing in the light.

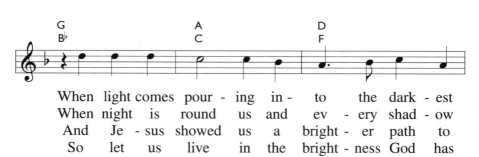

When light comes pour - ing in - to   the dark - est
When night is round us and   ev - ery shad - ow
And Je - sus showed us a   bright - er path to
So let us live in the   bright - ness God has

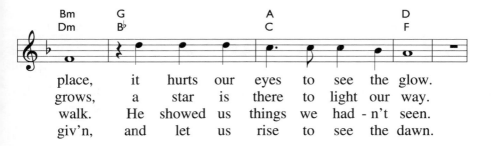

place,   it   hurts   our   eyes   to   see   the   glow.
grows,   a   star   is   there   to   light our   way.
walk.   He   showed us   things we   had - n't   seen.
giv'n,   and   let   us   rise   to   see   the   dawn.

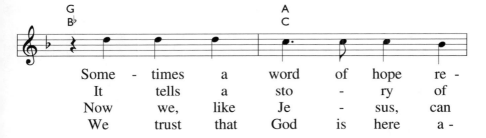

Some - times   a   word   of   hope   re -
It   tells   a   sto   - ry   of
Now   we, like Je - sus, can
We   trust   that God   is   here   a -

minds   us   of   our   fears,   our
Je - sus who came   near   to   say: "God's
help   cre - a - tion shine,   and
spar - kle and   a - blaze,

mem - or - ies and   tears.
light   will   ev - er   stay."
this   will   be   a   sign:
warm - ing   all   our   days.

Words: Linnea Good
Music: Linnea Good
Words and music copyright © 1992 Borealis Music.

Lord, Make Me an Alleluia

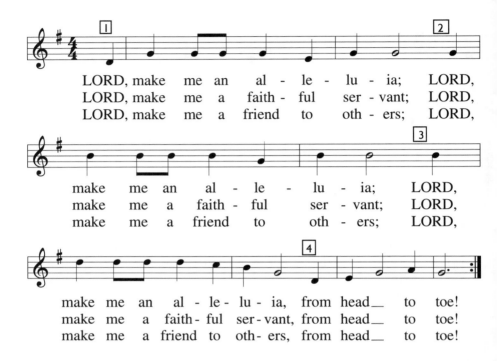

LORD, make me an al - le - lu - ia; LORD,
LORD, make me a faith - ful ser - vant; LORD,
LORD, make me a friend to oth - ers; LORD,

make me an al - le - lu - ia; LORD,
make me a faith - ful ser - vant; LORD,
make me a friend to oth - ers; LORD,

make me an al - le - lu - ia, from head__ to toe!
make me a faith - ful ser - vant, from head__ to toe!
make me a friend to oth - ers, from head__ to toe!

Words: Rae E. Whitney (based on words of Augustine of Hippo), 1987
Music: Ray W. Urwin, 1994

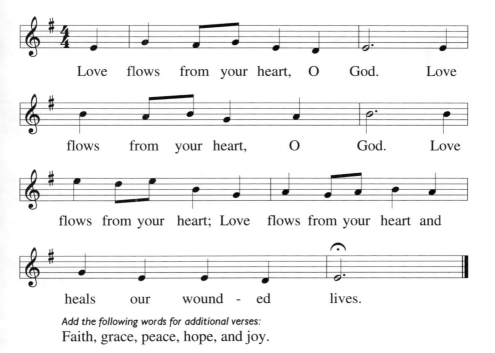

Love flows from your heart, O God. Love

flows from your heart, O God. Love

flows from your heart; Love flows from your heart and

heals our wound - ed lives.

Add the following words for additional verses:
Faith, grace, peace, hope, and joy.

Words: Flora & Wayne
Music: Flora & Wayne
Words and music copyright © 1998 Flora Litt & Wayne Irwin.

Make a Joyful Noise All the Earth

Make a joy - ful noise all the earth!

Wor - ship your God with glad - ness.

Make a joy - ful noise all the earth,

Come to this place with a song!

Know that your God has made you.
En - ter these gates, thanks giv - ing.
A - ges through end - less a - ges,

Know   it's   to   God   we   be - long.   And
En - ter these courts   with praise.   Sing
sea - sons of   end - less years,   the

come   to   this place with joy - ful - ness and praise.
thanks to your God   and bless this ho - ly Name.
love   of   our Ma - ker ev - er shall en - dure.

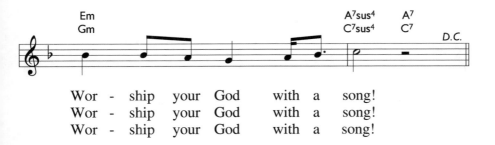

Wor - ship your God   with a   song!
Wor - ship your God   with a   song!
Wor - ship your God   with a   song!

Words: Linnea Good
Music: Linnea Good
Words and music copyright © 1991 Borealis Music.

My Lord, He Is A-comin' Soon

My Lord, he is a-com-in' soon; pre-

pare ye the way of the Lord._____ Get

ev-'ry-thing read - y for___ that day; pre-

pare ye the way of the Lord.

Words: L. Winnen & J. Cothran
Music: L. Winnen & J. Cothran

Words: Kevin Routledge
Music: Kevin Routledge
Copyright © 1975 Sovereign Music UK, Leighton Buzzard Beds, UK.

New Earth, Heavens New

Tune: Alexandra

Capo 3 D   Em/D   D   A   F#m   G

New __ earth,   heav - ens new,   Spir - it   of   God __
New __ love,   mer - cies new,   Spir - it   of   God __
New __ minds,   wis - dom new,   Spir - it   of   God __
New __ earth,   heav - ens new,   Spir - it   of   God __

Asus⁴   A   D   Em/D   D   A   F#m   G

mov-ing;   new __ seed, crea - tures new,   Spir-it   of   life __
mov-ing;   new __ strength, hope - ful - ness new,   Spir-it   of   life __
mov-ing;   new __ law,   cov - e - nant new,   Spir-it   of   life __
mov-ing;   new __ birth, crea - tures new,   Spir-it   of   life __

Asus⁴   A   G   D/F#   G   D/F#   Em   G

mov-ing;   new __ man wo - man new, im-age of God __ mov - ing.
mov-ing;   new __ hearts, spir - its new, im-age of God __ mov - ing.
mov-ing;   new __ name, na - ture new, im-age of God __ mov - ing.
mov-ing;   new __ men, wo - men new, im-age of God __ mov - ing.

D   Em/D   D   A   F#m
Refrain

Sing a new song to the One who has said, "Be - hold,

C   D   G/D   F#m/D   Em/D   D   Am⁷   A
    |1.-3. |4.

I make all things new."   new."

Words: Harris Loewen
Music: Harris Loewen

Ocean Is a Call to Worship

Tune: Santa Cruz

O-cean is a call to wor-ship ev - ery morn-ing, eve - ning;
in its ris - ing, fall - ing, hear the Spir - it breath-ing.

When your peo - ple scat - ter,
When our tem - ples tot - ter,
When I'm lis - tening, walk - ing,

bro - ken, bruised, and bat - tered,
Christ of wind and wa - ter,
pray - ing needs no talk - ing;

whis - per on the waves and call us home.
calm the earth and soothe our shat - tered nerves.
won - der at the depth and breadth of love.

Words: Daniel Charles Damon
Music: Daniel Charles Damon

54 *Oh, How He Loves You and Me*

Words: Kurt Kaiser/Word Music
Music: Kurt Kaiser/Word Music

Tune: Cantad Al Señor

Oh, sing to our God, oh, sing out a new song. Oh,
Oh, dance for our God and blow all the trum- pets. Oh,
Oh, shout to our God, who gave us the Spir - it. Oh,

sing to our God, oh, sing out a new song. Oh,
dance for our God and blow all the trum - pets. Oh,
shout to our God, who gave us the Spir - it. Oh,

sing to our God, oh, sing out a new song. Oh,
dance for our God and blow all the trum- pets. And
shout to our God, who gave us the Spir - it. Oh,

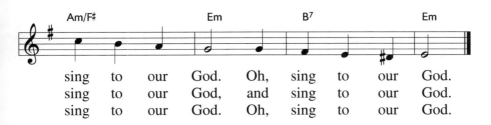

sing to our God. Oh, sing to our God.
sing to our God, and sing to our God.
sing to our God. Oh, sing to our God.

Words: Brazilian folk song, trans. Gerhard Cartford
Arrangement: John Bell

56

Peace

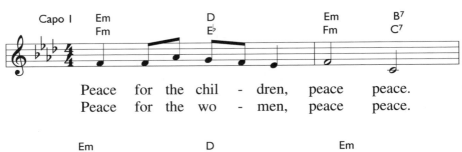

Peace for the chil - dren, peace peace.
Peace for the wo - men, peace peace.

Peace for the chil - dren we pray.
Peace for the wo - men we pray.

Fol - low - ing the path __ of One of peace, we
Fol - low - ing the path __ of One of peace, we

work for heal - ing, we work for peace;
work for heal - ing, we work for peace;

peace   for   the   chil - dren   to   -   day.
peace   for   the   wo - men   to   -   day.

3. Peace for the men...
4. Peace for our families..
5. Peace for the nations...
6. Peace for the creatures...
7. Peace for our planet...

8. Peace in the universe...
9. *Hum this verse softly, during which time individuals may call out the word "peace" in other languages, making a global connection.*
10. Peace in the soul...

Words: Doreen Lankshear-Smith
Music: Doreen Lankshear-Smith
Arrangement: David Abramsky
Words and music copyright © 1993 Doreen Lankshear-Smith. Arrangement copyright © 1998 David Abramsky.

57 *Oh, What a Wonderful Gift*

Oh what a won-der-ful gift! Oh what a

won-der-ful gift! God gives lives of hope and love,

Oh, what a won - der - ful gift!

Last time to Coda

"A -rise, your light has come!" The
To - day we bring a light, as
For all that we re - ceive, for
So, as we bring our gifts, and

world in still - ness lay, to hear the songs that
Ad - vent comes a - new, but hope and peace and
all the love we hold, we an - swer with our
of - fer them with pray'r, may we be peo - ple

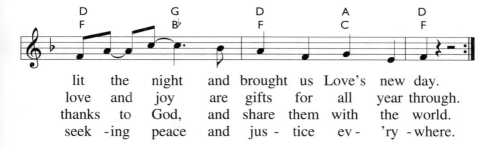

| D | | G | D | A | D |
| F | | B♭ | F | C | F |

lit   the   night   and brought us Love's new day.
love   and   joy   are gifts for   all year through.
thanks to   God,   and share them with the world.
seek -ing   peace   and jus - tice ev - 'ry -where.

| | D | Bm | A | G | A |
| CODA | F | Dm | C | B♭ | C |

Oh, what a won-der - ful,   Oh what a won-der - ful,

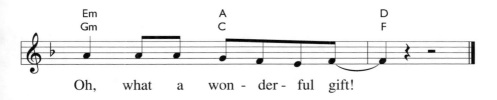

| Em | A | D |
| Gm | C | F |

Oh,   what   a   won - der - ful gift!

Words: Linnea Good
Music: Linnea Good
Words and music copyright © 1992 Borealis Music.

58 *One Bread, One Body*

One bread,   one bod - y,   one Lord of all,

one cup   of   bless - ing which we   bless;   and

we,   though ma - ny,   through - out   the earth,

we are one bod - y in this one   Lord.

Gen - tile   or   Jew,   ser - vant   or   free,
Ma - ny   the   gifts,   ma - ny   the   works,
Grain for the fields,   scat - tered and grown,

wom - an   or   man,   no   more.
one   in   the   Lord   of   all.
gath - ered to   one,   for   all.

Words: John B. Foley, SJ
Music: John B. Foley, SJ
Words and music copyright © 1978 John B. Foley SJ and New Dawn Music, Portland, OR. All rights reserved. Used by permission.

One God Created All That Is
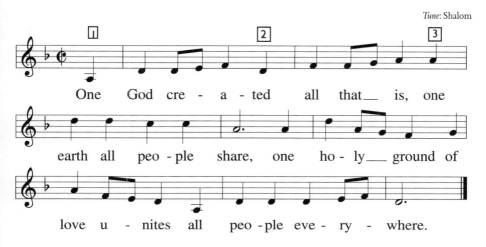

Tune: Shalom

One God cre - a - ted all that___ is, one
earth all peo - ple share, one ho - ly___ ground of
love u - nites all peo - ple eve - ry - where.

Words: Daniel Charles Damon *Music:* Israeli melody, adapted by Daniel Charles Damon

Praise Him!

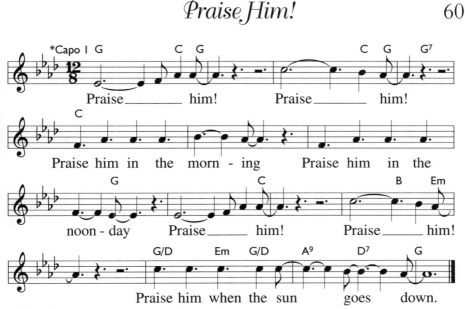

Praise_____ him! Praise_____ him!
Praise him in the morn - ing Praise him in the
noon - day Praise_____ him! Praise_____ him!
Praise him when the sun goes down.

The chords are for the use of guitarists only.

To create additional verses

Replace "Praise him" with love him, serve him, thank him, and Jesus

Words: African-American spiritual *Music:* African-American spiritual

Prepare the Way of the Lord

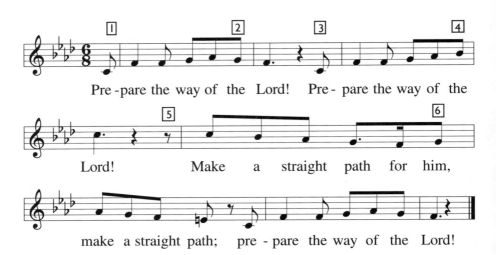

Pre -pare the way of the Lord! Pre - pare the way of the

Lord!   Make   a   straight   path   for   him,

make a straight path;   pre - pare the way of the Lord!

Words: Isaiah 40:3, adapt. Michael Burkhardt 1990
Music: Michael Burkhardt 1990
Words and music copyright © 1992 MorningStar Music Publishers. Used by permission.

Receive the Light of Christ

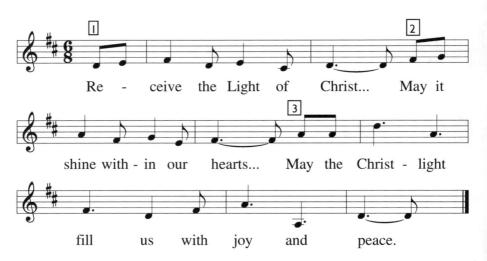

Re   -   ceive the Light   of   Christ...   May it

shine with - in our   hearts...   May the Christ - light

fill   us   with   joy   and   peace.

Words: Erica Marshall RSM
Music: Erica Marshall RSM
Words and music copyright © 1994 E. Marshall, Willow Connection Pty Ltd., Sydney.

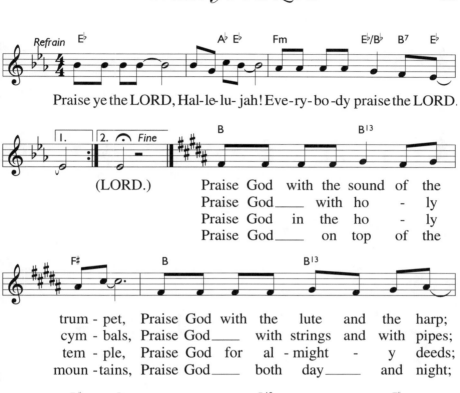

Praise ye the LORD, Hal-le-lu-jah! Eve-ry-bo-dy praise the LORD.

(LORD.)

Praise God with the sound of the
Praise God____ with ho - ly
Praise God in the ho - ly
Praise God____ on top of the

trum - pet, Praise God with the lute and the harp;
cym - bals, Praise God____ with strings and with pipes;
tem - ple, Praise God for al - might - y deeds;
moun -tains, Praise God____ both day____ and night;

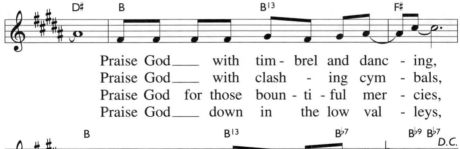

Praise God____ with tim - brel and danc - ing,
Praise God____ with clash - ing cym - bals,
Praise God for those boun - ti - ful mer - cies,
Praise God____ down in the low val - leys,

Praise God wher - ev - er you are.
Praise God with all of your might.
For God ful - fills____ our needs.
Praise God be - cause it's al - right.

Words: Paul J. Cleveland
Music: Paul J. Cleveland
Words and music copyright © 1981 Paul Jefferson Cleveland. All rights reserved. Used by permission.

Sanna, Sannanina

San - na san -na-ni - na, san - na, san - na, san - na,
San - na, san - na - ni - na, san - na, san - na, san - na
San - na, san -na, san - na, san-na - ni - na,
san - na, san - na, san - na San - na, san - na, san -
na, san - na - ni - na, san - na, san - na, san - na.

Words: traditional South African
Music: traditional South African
Arrangement: Nicholas Williams

Spirit of Life

Spir - it of Life, come un - to me. Sing in my

heart all the stir - rings of com - pas - sion. Blow in the

wind, rise in the sea; move in the hand, giv - ing

life the shape of jus - tice. Roots hold me close; wings set me

free; Spir - it of Life, come to me, come to me.

Words: Carolyn McDade 1981
Music: Carolyn McDade 1981
Harmony: Grace Lewis-McLaren

Sing a New Song

Refrain

Sing a new song un-to the LORD; let your song be sung from moun-tains high. Sing a new song un-to the LORD, sing-ing "Al - le - lu - ia."
*praise for ev - er.

Verses

Yah - weh's peo - ple dance for joy; O come be -
Rise, O chil - dren, from your sleep; your Sav - ior
Glad my soul for I have seen the glo - ry

fore the LORD. And play for him on glad tam - bou -
now has come. He has turned your sor - row to
of the LORD. The trum - pet sounds; the dead shall be

rines, and let your trum - pet sound.
joy, and filled your soul with song.
raised. I know my Sav - ior lives.

alternate text for the Lenten season

Words: Daniel Schutte   *Music:* Daniel Schutte

Slow Me Down

Words: Jack Walker
Music: Jack Walker
Words and music copyright © 1996 Jack Walker.

Spirit Song

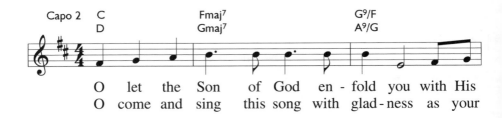

O let the Son of God en - fold you with His
O come and sing this song with glad - ness as your

Spir - it and His love. Let Him fill your life and
hearts are filled with joy. Lift your hands in sweet sur-

sat - is - fy your soul. O let Him have the things that
ren - der to His name. O give Him all your tears and

hold you and His Spir - it, like a dove, will des-
sad - ness, give Him all your years of pain and you'll

cend up - on your life and make you whole.
en - ter in - to life in Je - sus' Name.

Je - sus, O Je - sus, come and fill Your lambs. ___

Je - sus, O Je - sus, come and fill Your lambs.

Words: John Wimber
Music: John Wimber

Words and music copyright © 1979 Mercy/Vineyard Publishing.

69 The Spring Has Come

Tune: Vervacity

The spring has come, let all the church be
The sun is warm, let all God's chil - dren
The spring has come, new peo - ple are the

part of it! The world has
play in it! The world ex -
flowers of it. Through wind and

changed, and God is at the heart of it!
pands, let's spread the Gos - pel way in it!
rain, new life is in the showers of it.

New light, new day, new col - or aft - er
New leaf, new thrust, new green - ing for the
New bud, new shoot, new hope will bear the

win - ter gray. New light, new day, the spring has
love of Christ. New leaf, new thrust, the sun is
Spir - it's fruit. New bud, new shoot, the spring has

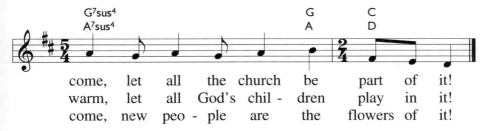

come, let all the church be part of it!
warm, let all God's chil - dren play in it!
come, new peo - ple are the flowers of it!

Words: Shirley Erena Murray
Music: Colin Gibson
Words and music copyright © 1992 by Hope Publishing Co., Carol Stream, IL 60188. All rights reserved. Used by permission.

Take Me to the Water 70

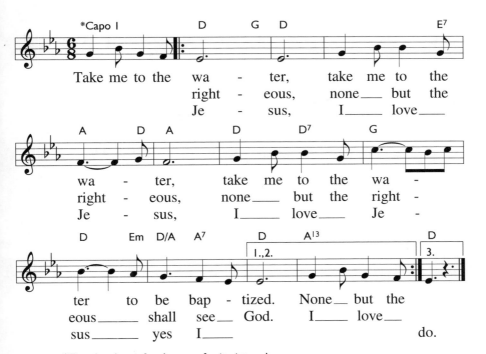

Take me to the wa - ter, take me to the
right - eous, none ___ but the
Je - sus, I ___ love ___

wa - ter, take me to the wa -
right - eous, none ___ but the right -
Je - sus, I ___ love ___ Je -

ter to be bap - tized. None ___ but the
eous ___ shall see ___ God. I ___ love ___
sus ___ yes I ___ do.

*The chords are for the use of guitarists only.

Words: African-American spiritual   *Music:* African-American spiritual
Arrangement in the African-American gospel music style of Willie P. Dorsey, Sr. Arrangement copyright © 1998
Professional Music Services, Inc., New Orleans, LA. All rights reserved. Used by permission.

Teach Me Lord to Wait

They that wait up - on the LORD shall re - new their

strength; they shall mount up with wings __ as ea - gles;

They shall run and not be wea - ry; They shall

walk and not __ faint; Teach me, LORD, Teach me,

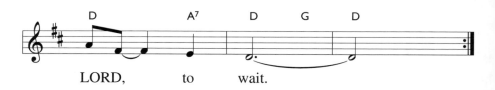

LORD, to wait.

Words: Stuart Hamblen
Music: Stuart Hamblen
Words and music copyright © 1953 Hamblen Music, renewed 1981.

There's Room at the Table

Tune: Love Feast

The bread and the wine are here; come now all who— hun - ger and thirst. Come need - y, come now with - out— fear. Drink joy, as the last be -come first! Come in, sit down,— there's room at the ta - ble; en - joy the feast Love has spread— for you.

Words: Daniel Charles Damon
Music: Daniel Charles Damon
Words and music copyright © 1993 by Hope Publishing Co., Carol Stream, IL 60188. All rights reserved. Used by permission.

73 *This Joy I Have*

*The chords are for the use of guitarists only.

For additional verses use:
Hope, peace, and love

Words: African–American spiritual
Music: African–American spiritual
Arrangement in the African–American gospel music style of Willie P. Dorsey, Sr.
Arrangement copyright © 1998 Professional Music Services, Inc., New Orleans, LA. All rights reserved. Used by permission.

There's a song of love in my heart; love is a gift from Je - sus. There's a song of love in my heart; love is a gift from God.

Refrain
Al - le - lu - ia! Love in my heart is sing-ing prais - es.

Al - le - lu - ia! Love is a gift from God.

In stanzas 2 - 5 replace the word "love" with

2. Peace   4. Hope

3. Faith   5. Joy

Remember to replace "love" in the refrain as well.

Words: Handt Hanson
Music: Handt Hanson
Piano adaptation: Henry Wiens

We Meet Together for Peace

We meet to - geth- er for peace; we
pray to - geth- er for peace. From ma - ny cul - tures,
faiths and lands we join our voic - es join our hands, to
work to - geth - er for peace, to work to -geth - er for peace.

Words: Doreen Lankshear-Smith   *Music:* Doreen Lankshear-Smith   *Arrangement:* Sue Swanson
Words and music copyright © 1993 Doreen Lankshear-Smith. Arrangement copyright © 1998 Sue Swanson.

76

This Li'l Light of Mine

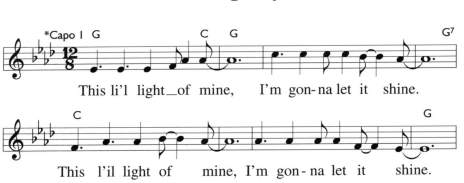

This li'l light—of mine, I'm gon-na let it shine.
This l'il light of mine, I'm gon-na let it shine.

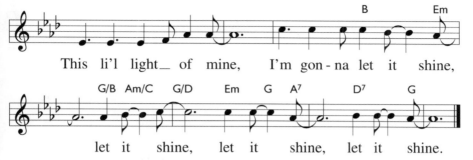

This li'l light__ of mine, I'm gon-na let it shine,

let it shine, let it shine, let it shine.

2. Everywhere I go...
3. Jesus gave it to me...

Words: African–American spiritual *Music:* African–American spiritual
Arrangement in the African-American gospel music style of Willie P. Dorsey, Sr. Arrangement copyright © 1998
Professional Music Services, Inc., New Orleans, LA. All rights reserved. Used by permission.

This Li'l Light of Mine 77

This li'l light of mine_____ I'm gon-na let it shine.

Oh__ This li'l light of mine_____ I'm gon-na let it shine.

This li'l light of mine_____ I'm gon-na let it shine

Let it shine, let it shine, let it shine.

See #76 for additional stanzas.

Words: African–American spiritual *Music:* African–American spiritual
Arrangement in the African-American gospel music style of Willie P. Dorsey, Sr. Arrangement copyright © 1998
Professional Music Services, Inc., New Orleans, LA. All rights reserved. Used by permission.

We Are One

Tune: We Are One

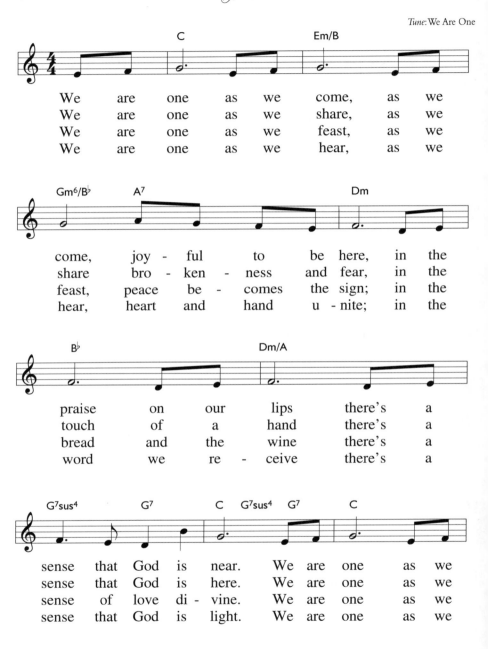

	C				Em/B		
We	are	one	as	we	come,	as	we
We	are	one	as	we	share,	as	we
We	are	one	as	we	feast,	as	we
We	are	one	as	we	hear,	as	we

Gm⁶/B♭ — A⁷ — Dm

come,	joy - ful	to	be here,	in	the
share,	bro - ken - ness	and	fear,	in	the
feast,	peace be - comes	the	sign;	in	the
hear,	heart and hand	u - nite;	in	the	

B♭ — Dm/A

praise	on	our	lips	there's	a
touch	of	a	hand	there's	a
bread	and	the	wine	there's	a
word	we	re - ceive	there's	a	

G⁷sus⁴ — G⁷ — C — G⁷sus⁴ — G⁷ — C

sense	that God is	near.	We are one	as we
sense	that God is	here.	We are one	as we
sense	of love di - vine.	We are one	as we	
sense	that God is	light.	We are one	as we

Em			Gm		C⁷		F		
sing,	as	we	seek,	we	are	found,	and	we
care,	as	we	heal,	we	are	healed;	and	we
come,	as	we	feed,	we	are	fed;	and	we
leave,	as	we	love,	we	are	loved;	and	we

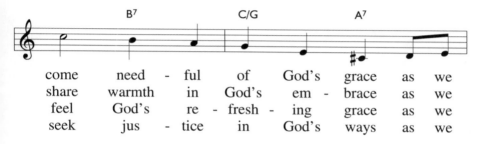

	B⁷			C/G		A⁷		
come	need - ful	of	God's	grace	as	we
share	warmth	in	God's	em - brace	as	we
feel	God's	re - fresh - ing	grace	as	we
seek	jus - tice	in	God's	ways	as	we

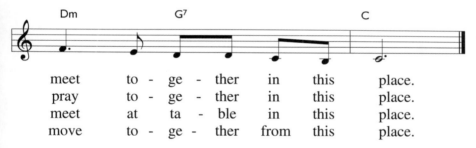

Dm		G⁷			C		
meet	to - ge - ther	in	this	place.
pray	to - ge - ther	in	this	place.
meet	at ta - ble	in	this	place.
move	to - ge - ther	from	this	place.

Words: Doreen Lankshear-Smith
Music: Jeeva Sam
Arrangement: David Kai
Words copyright © 1988 Doreen Lankshear-Smith. Music copyright © 1987 Jeeva Sam.
Arrangement copyright © 1995 David Kai.

79

We Praise You, God

Tune: Applegate

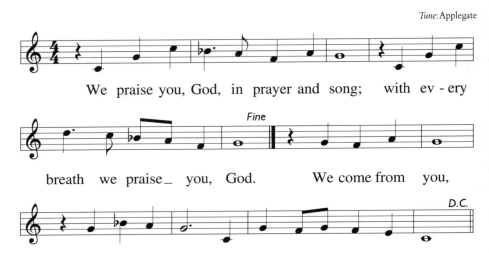

We praise you, God, in prayer and song; with ev - ery

Fine

breath we praise_ you, God.   We come from   you,

D.C.

we live in   you,   O   God, we re - turn to   you.

Words: Daniel Charles Damon
Music: Daniel Charles Damon

Siyahamba

We are march - ing in the
Si - ya - hamb' e - ku - kha -

light of God, we are march-ing in the light of
nyen' kwen - khos', si - ya -hamb' e - ku - kha -nyen' kwen-

God. We are march - ing, oo,_____ we are
khos'. Si - ya - ham - ba, oo,_____ si - ya -

march - ing in the light of God.
hamb', e - ku - kha - nyen' kwen khos'.

Words: South African traditional, trans. Anders Nyberg 1984
Music: South African traditional, arr. Anders Nyberg
Translation and arrangement copyright © 1984 Walton Music Corporation.

What Does the Lord Require

Tune: Moon

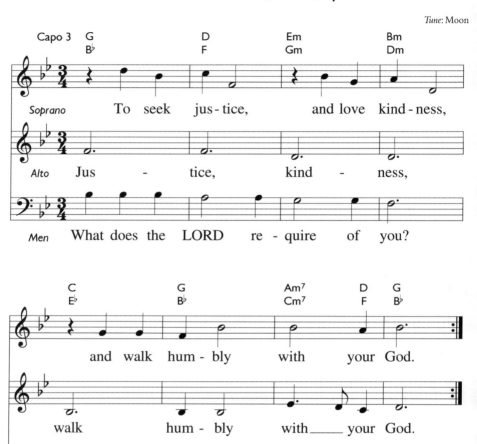

Words: Micah 6:8
Music: Jim Strathdee
Copyright © 1986 by Desert Flower Music, Carmichael, CA.

Weave

Words: Rosemary Crow
Music: Rosemary Crow
Words and music copyright © 1979 Rosemary Crow.

When I Rose This Morning

When I rose this morn-in' I didn't have no doubt.

When I rose this morn-in' I didn't have no doubt.

When I rose this morn-in' I didn't have no doubt.

I didn't have no doubt in my mind.

*The chords are for the use of guitarists only.

2. When I saw the bright sunshine, I didn't have no doubt...
3. When I got down on my knees, I didn't have no doubt...
4. No doubt, no doubt, I didn't have no doubt...

Words: African–American spiritual
Music: African–American spiritual
Arrangement in the African-American gospel music style of Willie P. Dorsey, Sr.
Arrangement copyright © 1998 Professional Music Services, Inc., New Orleans, LA.
All rights reserved. Used by permission.

When We Pray

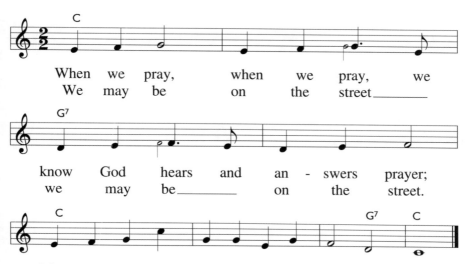

When we pray, when we pray, we
We may be on the street_____

know God hears and an - swers prayer;
we may be_____ on the street.

Mat - ters not where we may be, God an - swers prayer.

Add your own verses. Some suggestions are
We may be in a church...
We may be in a park...
We may be at the lake...
We may be on the job...
We may be sick in bed...

Words: Jeeva Sam
Music: Jeeva Sam
Words and music copyright © 1997 Jeeva Sam.

Alleluia Round

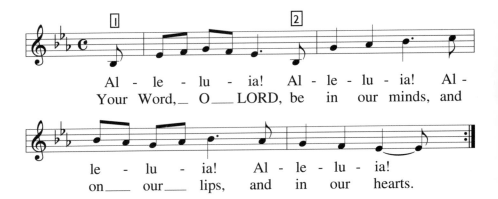

Al - le - lu - ia! Al - le - lu - ia! Al -
Your Word,__ O__ LORD, be in our minds, and

le - lu - ia! Al - le - lu - ia!
on__ our__ lips, and in our hearts.

Words: Carey Landry *Music:* Carey Landry

Are Not Our Hearts

Are not our hearts burn - ing with - in us. Are not our

hearts light - ed with fire. Je - sus is with us, is ris - en, is

with us, Je - sus is ris - en, is with us to - day. Je -

sus is the Lord! Je - sus is__ the Lord.

Words: Carey Landry *Music:* Carey Landry

Woke up this morn - in' with my mind and it was

stayed on Je -sus, woke up this morn - in' with my mind_

stayed on the Lawd,__ woke up this morn - in' with my

mind and it was stayed on Je -sus, hal - le -

lu, hal - le - lu hal - le - lu - jah.

*The chords are for the use of guitarists only.

2. Singin' and prayin' with my mind...
3. Walkin' and talkin' with my mind...

Words: African–American spiritual
Music: African–American spiritual
Arrangement in the African-American gospel music style of Willie P. Dorsey, Sr.
Arrangement copyright © 1998 Professional Music Services, Inc., New Orleans, LA. All rights reserved. Used by permission.

88 *You Nourish Us*

You nour-ish us with food, O__ God, for bod-y and for soul; our love and ser-vice__ is our__ thanks, for life that's free and whole,_____ for life that's__ free and whole.

Words: Flora & Wayne
Music: Nikolaus Herman 1554, harm. Johann Sebastian Bach
Words copyright © 1979 Flora Litt & Wayne Irwin.

89 *Where Streams Run Dry*

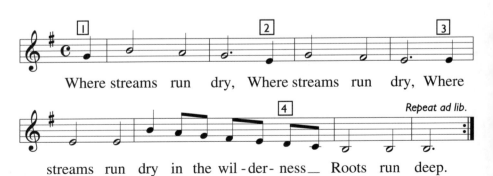

Where streams run dry, Where streams run dry, Where streams run dry in the wil-der-ness__ Roots run deep.

Words: Linnea Good
Music: Linnea Good
Words and music copyright © 1994 Borealis Music.

The Bell Song

1. & 5. You got-ta have love   in your heart.   You got-ta have
              peace   on your mind.   You got-ta have
              joy   in your soul.   You got-ta have
              la   la   la   la etc.

love   in your heart.   You knew it was__ Je - sus
peace   on your mind.   You knew it was__ Je - sus
joy   in your soul.   The love__ of__ Je - sus

right from the   start.   You got - ta have love
there all   the   time.   You got - ta have peace
will make you   whole.   You got - ta have joy

in your heart.   2. You   got - ta have
on your mind.   3. You   got - ta have
in your soul.   4. La   la   la   la

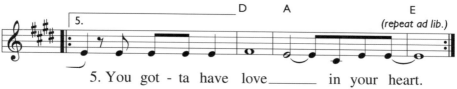

5. You got - ta have love_____ in your heart.

Words: David Lynch
Music: David Lynch
Words and music copyright © 1976 David Lynch.

Night Has Fallen

Night has fall - en, night has
Dark - ness now has come, dark - ness
We are with_____ you, we are
You have kept_____ us, you have
See your chil - dren, see your
Keep us in Your love, keep us
Now we go to rest, now we

Capo 3

D	A	D	A
F	C	F	C

Refrain

fall - en,
now has come,
with_____ you
kept_____ us,   grac - ious   Spir - it,
chil - dren,
in Your love,
go to rest,

Em	D	Em	Bm	G	D
Gm	F	Gm	Dm	B♭	F

guard us sleep - ing.

Words: Tom Colvin
Music: Tom Colvin

Come, Let Us Seek

Tune: Chilema

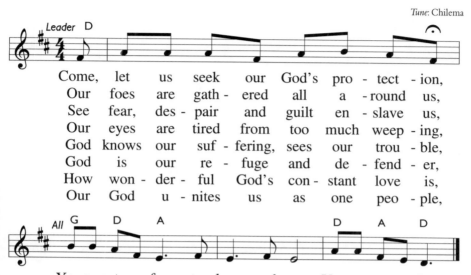

Come, let us seek our God's pro - tect - ion,
Our foes are gath - ered all a - round us,
See fear, des - pair and guilt en - slave us,
Our eyes are tired from too much weep - ing,
God knows our suf - fering, sees our trou - ble,
God is our re - fuge and de - fend - er,
How won - der - ful God's con - stant love is,
Our God u - nites us as one peo - ple,

Ye - su sets us free to love and serve, Ye - su sets us free.

Additional verses:
Let's dance and sing to God our Savior...
And shout for joy with all God's children...
Haleluya, yes, haleluya...

Words: Tom Colvin   *Music:* Tom Colvin

You Who Love God

You who love God lift your hands and praise God.

You who love God lift your hands and pray.

Words: Jack Miffleton   *Music:* Jack Miffleton

94   *Fear Not, for I Have Redeemed You*

Refrain G⁷   C   F   Dm

Fear   not,   for   I   have   re - deemed___   you;

G   G⁷   C   Dm⁷ G⁷   C

I   have called   you   by   name.   I   have

C⁷   F   Dm   G   Dm⁷ G⁷ C   C⁷   C

To verses | *Final*

called   you   by   name;_____   you   are   mine. __

Verses   F   G⁷

1. When you   pass   through the   wa - ters   I   will___
2. Be - cause   you   are   pre - cious   and   I___
3.   You   are   my   wit - ness - es;   I   have
4. It's___ time   now   to   lay   a - side   the___
5. The___ riv - ers   that   flow___   in   the___

C   Am   Dm

be   with   you;   and through riv - ers,   they will
love___ you,   you   whom   I___
cho - sen   you   that   you   may___
for - mer   things;   a___   new   day   has___
des - ert   give___ drink___   to___

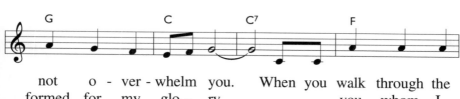

not	o - ver - whelm	you.	When you	walk	through	the
formed	for	my	glo -	ry,		you	whom	I
know	and	be - lieve	me.		You	are	my
dawned,	do	you	see	it?	I'm___	mak - ing	a
my	cho - sen	peo - ple,	to___	quench___	their

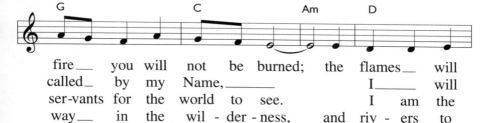

fire___	you will	not	be	burned;	the	flames___	will
called_	by	my	Name,_____		I_____	will
ser-vants	for	the	world	to	see.		I	am	the
way_	in	the	wil - der - ness,	and	riv - ers	to
thirst_	and	to	strength - en	them,	that	they___	might

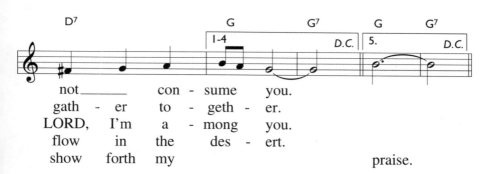

not_____	con - sume	you.
gath - er	to - geth - er.
LORD, I'm	a - mong	you.
flow	in	the	des - ert.
show	forth	my		praise.

Words: Isaiah 43:1-21, adapted Jodi Page-Clark
Music: Jodi Page-Clark

95

Be Not Afraid

Verses

G Gsus⁴ G Gsus⁴

1. You shall cross the bar-ren des- ert, but you
2. If you pass through rag-ing wa-ters in the
3. Bless-ed are your poor, for the

G Gsus⁴ G D/F# C Csus²

shall not die of thirst. You shall wan-der far in
sea, you shall not drown. If you walk a-mid the
King-dom shall be theirs. Blest are you that

C C/B Am Am/G D/F#

safe-ty though you do not know the way. You shall
burn-ing flames, you shall not be harmed. If you
weep and mourn, for one day you shall laugh. And if

speak your words in for-eign lands and all will un-der-
stand be-fore the pow'r of hell and death is at your
wick-ed tongues in-sult and hate you all be-cause of
stand. You shall see the face of God and live.
side, know that I am with you through it all.
Me, bless-ed, bless-ed are you!

Refrain
Be not a-fraid. I go be-fore you al-ways. Come, fol-low
Me, and I will give you rest.

Words: Based on Isaiah 43:2-3, Luke 6:20ff, Bob Dufford, SJ
Music: Bob Dufford, SJ
Words and music copyright © 1975, 1978 Robert J. Dufford, SJ and New Dawn Music, Portland, OR.
All rights reserved. Used with permission.

The Foot Washing Song

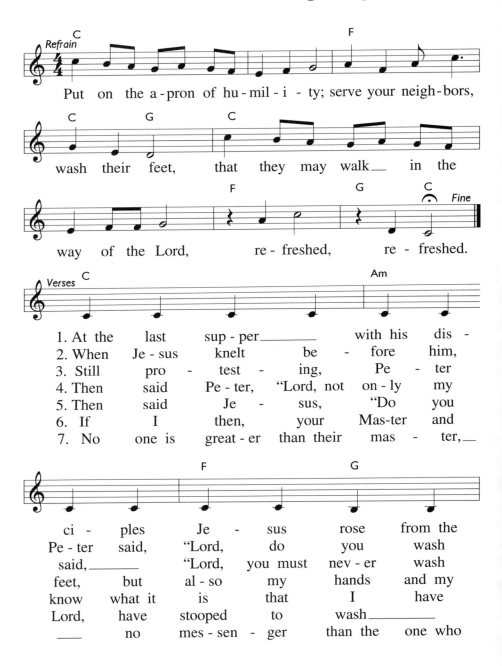

Put on the a-pron of hu-mil-i-ty; serve your neigh-bors, wash their feet, that they may walk in the way of the Lord, re-freshed, re-freshed.

Verses

1. At the last sup-per with his dis-ci-ples Je-sus rose from the
2. When Je-sus knelt be-fore him, Pe-ter said, "Lord, do you wash
3. Still pro-test-ing, Pe-ter said, "Lord, you must nev-er wash
4. Then said Pe-ter, "Lord, not on-ly my feet, but al-so my hands and my
5. Then said Je-sus, "Do you know what it is that I have
6. If I then, your Mas-ter and Lord, have stooped to wash
7. No one is great-er than their mas-ter, no mes-sen-ger than the one who

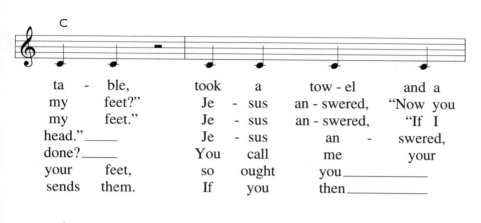

ta	- ble,	took	a	tow - el	and a
my	feet?"	Je	- sus	an - swered,	"Now you
my	feet."	Je	- sus	an - swered,	"If I
head."		Je	- sus	an -	swered,
done?		You	call	me	your
your	feet,	so	ought	you	
sends	them.	If	you	then	

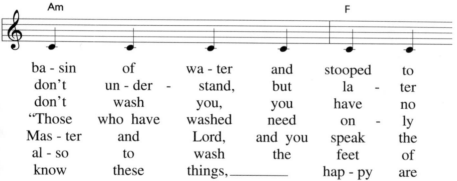

ba - sin	of	wa - ter	and	stooped	to
don't	un - der -	stand,	but	la - ter
don't	wash	you,	you	have	no
"Those	who have	washed	need	on - ly
Mas - ter	and	Lord,	and you	speak	the
al - so	to	wash	the	feet	of
know	these	things,		hap - py	are

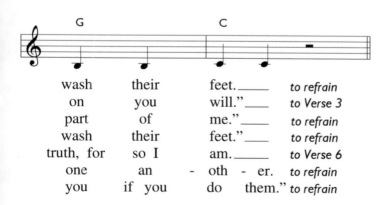

wash	their	feet.	*to refrain*
on	you	will."	*to Verse 3*
part	of	me."	*to refrain*
wash	their	feet."	*to refrain*
truth, for	so I	am.	*to Verse 6*
one	an -	oth - er.	*to refrain*
you	if you	do	them." *to refrain*

Words: John 13, adapted Shirley Lewis Brown
Music: Shirley Lewis Brown
Words and music copyright © 1972 GIA Publications, Inc. Used by permission.

I Will Call

Words: Victor Rubbo
Music: Victor Rubbo
Words and music copyright © 1982 Mercy/Vineyard Publishing.
All rights reserved. International copyright secured. Used by permission.

Everyone's Rejoicing

Eve - ry - one's re - joic - ing,
Chi - u - ta our mak - er
Chi - u - ta sent Ye - su,
Dear - ly Ye - su loves us,
Peace with jus - tice mak - ing
Come, Chi - u - ta's peo - ple,

eve - ry - one is sing - ing,
is the world's cre - a - tor.
chains and fet - ters break - ing,
sets his heart up - on us,
is the kind of lov - ing
come, we are to - geth - er,

prais - es to *Chi - u - ta, al - le - lu - ya.
For Chi - u - ta drums beat, al - le - lu - ya.
bless - ed free - dom giv - ing, al - le - lu - ya.
leads us to Chi - u - ta, al - le - lu - ya.
called for by Chi - u - ta, al - le - lu - ya.
one in Ye - su sing - ing al - le - lu - ya.

Refrain

A -men, al - le - lu - ya, a -men, al - le - lu - ya,

a -men, al - le - lu - ya, al - le - lu - ya.

*Chiuta (chee-oo-ta) is one name for God in Malawi.

Words: Tom Colvin
Music: Tom Colvin
Words and music copyright © 1997 by Hope Publishing Co., Carol Stream, IL 60188. All rights reserved. Used by permission.

Lay Your Hands Gently

Refrain

Capo 3

Lay your hands gent - ly up - on us.

Let their touch ren - der your peace.

Let them bring your for - give - ness and heal - ing.

Fine

Lay your hands gent - ly, lay your hands.

Verses

1. You were sent to free the bro - ken

2. Lord, we come to you through one an -

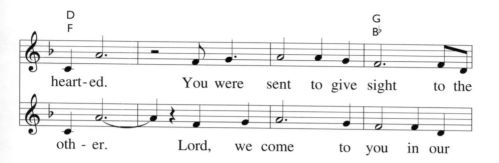

heart-ed.   You were   sent   to give sight   to the

oth - er.   Lord,   we come   to   you   in our

blind.   You de - sire   to heal   all our ill - ness -

need.   Lord, we come   to   you seek - ing   whole - ness.

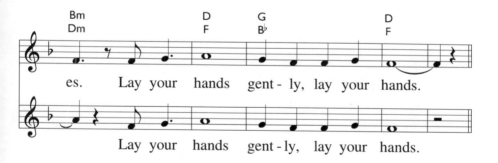

es.   Lay your   hands   gent - ly, lay your   hands.

Lay your   hands   gent - ly, lay your   hands.

Words: Carey Landry
Music: Carey Landry
Words and music copyright © 1977 North American Liturgy Resources (NALR), Portland, OR.
All rights reserved. Used with permission.

100

Make a Joyful Sound

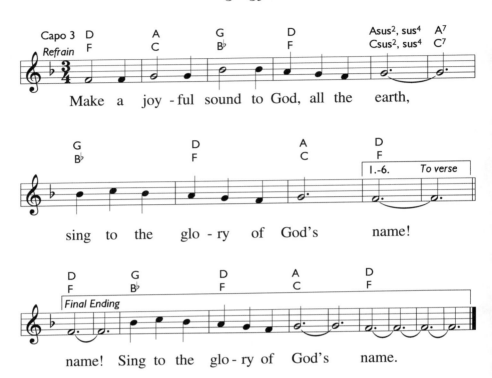

Make a joy - ful sound to God, all the earth,

sing to the glo - ry of God's name!

Final Ending

name! Sing to the glo - ry of God's name.

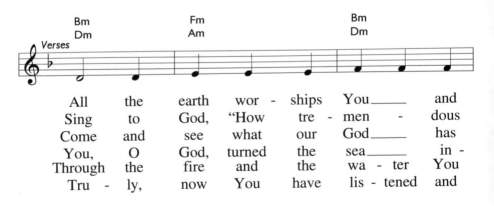

Verses

All	the	earth	wor -	ships	You_____	and
Sing	to	God,	"How	tre -	men -	dous
Come	and	see	what	our	God_____	has
You,	O	God,	turned	the	sea_____	in -
Through	the	fire	and	the	wa - ter	You
Tru -	ly,	now	You	have	lis - tened	and

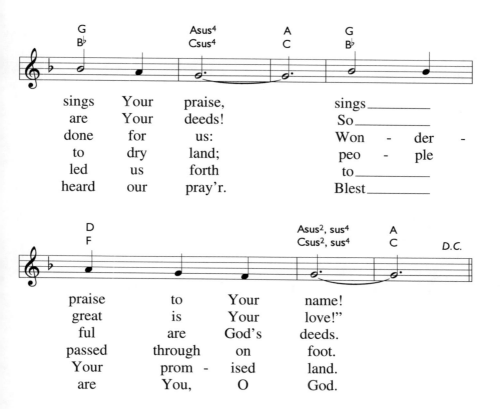

sings   Your   praise,   sings _____
are   Your   deeds!   So _____
done   for   us: Won - der -
to   dry   land;   peo - ple
led   us   forth   to _____
heard   our   pray'r.   Blest _____

praise   to   Your   name!
great   is   Your   love!"
ful   are   God's   deeds.
passed   through on   foot.
Your   prom - ised   land.
are   You,   O   God.

Words: Weston Priory & Mary David Callahan
Music: Weston Priory & Mary David Callahan

Only a Shadow

Capo 3

G / B♭

The love we have for you, O Lord, is ___
The Bread we take and eat, O Lord, is ___
Our own be - lief in you, O Lord, ___ is
The dreams we have to - day, O Lord, ___ are
The joy we share to - day, O Lord, ___ is

C / E♭   **G / B♭**

on - ly a ___ shad - ow of your love for us;
your bod - y ___ bro - ken and shared with us;
on - ly ___ a shad - ow of your faith in us;
on - ly ___ a shad - ow of your dreams for us;
on - ly ___ a shad - ow of your joys for us;

C / E♭   **G / B♭**

on - ly a shad - ow of your love for
your bod - y bro - ken and shared with
on - ly a shad - ow of your faith in
on - ly a shad - ow of your dreams for
on - ly a shad - ow of your joys for

us, your deep a - bid - ing love. *to vs. 2*
us, the gift of your great love. *to refrain*
us; your deep and last - ing faith. *to vs. 4*
us; if we but fol - low you. *to refrain*
us; when we meet face to face. *to refrain*

Refrain
Our lives are in your hands, our lives

are in your hands. Our love for you will

grow, O Lord; your light in us will shine. *Refrain goes to vs. 3, and 5.*

Words: Carey Landry
Music: Carey Landry
Words and music copyright © 1971 Carey Landry and
North American Liturgy Resources (NALR), Portland, OR. All rights reserved. Used with permission.

102

Song of the Body of Christ

We___ come to share our sto - ry, we___ come to break the bread, we___ come to know our ris - ing from the___ dead.

1. We_____ come as your
2. We are called to heal the

3. Bread of life and cup of
4. You will lead and we shall
5. We will live and sing your

peo - ple, we___ come as your own, u -
bro - ken, to be hope for the poor, we are

prom - ise, in this meal we all are one. In our
fol - low, you will be the breath of life; liv - ing
prais - es. "Al - le - lu - ia" is our song. May we

ni - ted with each oth - er, love finds a home.
called to feed the hun - gry at our___ door.

dy - ing and our ris - ing, may your king-dom come.
wa - ter, we are thirst - ing for___ your___ light.
live in love and peace our whole___ life___ long.

Words: David Haas
Music: Traditional Hawaiian, arr. David Haas
Words and music copyright © 1989 GIA Publications, Inc.

103

God of Mercy

Refrain

Capo 3: D / F — F#dim⁷ / Adim⁷ — G / B♭ — D/F# / F/A — Em / Gm — D/F# / F/A — A / C — Em/G / Gm/B♭

Hear our prayer. Hear our prayer.

F#m / Am — A⁷ / C⁷/G — G/D / B♭/F — D / F — D/A / F/C — A / C — D / F *Fine*

God of mer - cy, hear our prayer.

Verses

D / F — F#dim⁷ / Adim⁷ — G / B♭ — D/F# / F/A — Em / Gm — D/F# / F/A — A / C — Em/G / Gm/B♭

For all the church: may it be
Teach us to stand with all who
May we sup - port all those who

F#m / Am — A⁷ / C⁷/G — G/D / B♭/F — D / F — D/A / F/C — A / C — D G/D / F B♭/F

Christ's com - pas - sion.
know op - pres - sion. Hear our prayer.
work for jus - tice.

Words: Bob Hurd
Music: Bob Hurd
Words and music copyright © 1991 Bob Hurd. Published by OCP Publications.
All rights reserved. Used by permission.

Adoramus Te Domine

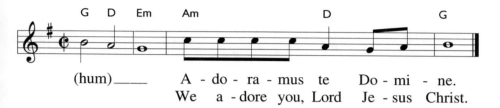

(hum)_____

A - do - ra - mus te Do - mi - ne.
We a - dore you, Lord Je - sus Christ.

Words: traditional
Translation: Taizé Community (France)
Music: Taizé Community (France)
Copyright © 1981 Les Presses de Taizé (France).
Used by permission of GIA Publications, Inc.

Stay with Me

Stay with me, re - main here with me,

watch__ and pray,__ watch and pray.

Words: from Matthew 26, Taizé Community (France)
Music: Taizé Community (France)
Copyright © 1991 Les Presses de Taizé (France).
Used by permission of GIA Publications, Inc.

106   *Ubi Caritas*

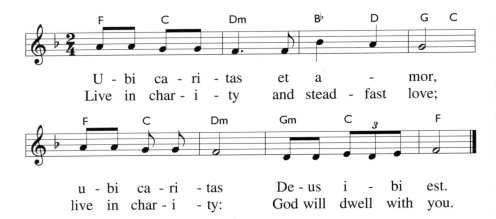

U - bi ca - ri - tas   et   a - mor,
Live in char - i - ty   and stead - fast   love;

u - bi ca - ri - tas   De - us   i - bi   est.
live in char - i - ty: God will dwell with you.

Words: traditional
Translation: Taizé Community (France)
Music: Taizé Community (France)
Copyright © 1991 Les Presses de Taizé (France).
Used by permission of GIA Publications, Inc.

107   *Wisdom Calls*

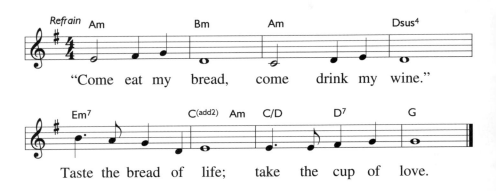

"Come eat my bread,   come   drink my wine."

Taste the bread of life;   take   the cup of love.

Words: Andrew Dreitcer
Music: Michael McCarty
Words copyright © 1997 Andrew Dreitcer.
Music copyright © 1997 Mimesis Press.

a. Jesus Christ, Son of God

Je-sus Christ, Son of God, make your-self known through me.

b. Jesus Christ, Son of the Living God

Je - sus Christ, Son of the liv-ing God, speak through

me to oth - ers. Je - sus

Words: Kevin R. Hackett
Music: Kevin R. Hackett
Words and music copyright © 1990 Celebration.
(Administered by The Copyright Company, Nashville, TN.)
All rights reserved. International copyright reserved. Used by permission.

109   *Come Holy Spirit, Come as a Dove*

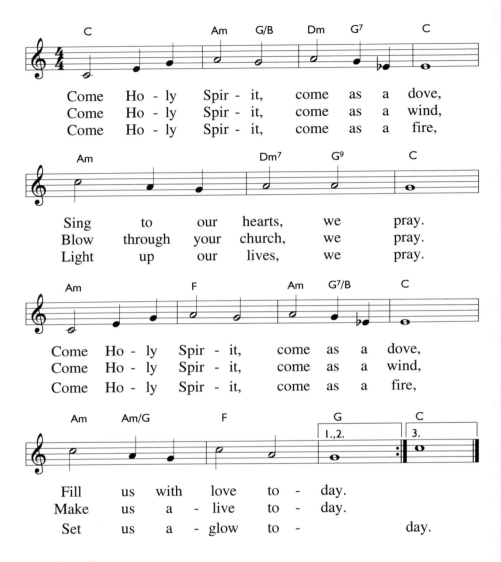

Come Ho - ly Spir - it, come as a dove,
Come Ho - ly Spir - it, come as a wind,
Come Ho - ly Spir - it, come as a fire,

Sing to our hearts, we pray.
Blow through your church, we pray.
Light up our lives, we pray.

Come Ho - ly Spir - it, come as a dove,
Come Ho - ly Spir - it, come as a wind,
Come Ho - ly Spir - it, come as a fire,

Fill us with love to - day.
Make us a - live to - day.
Set us a - glow to - day.

Words: Flora & Wayne
Music: Flora & Wayne
Words and music copyright © 1996, 1998 Flora Litt & Wayne Irwin.

Come Holy Spirit, I Need You

110

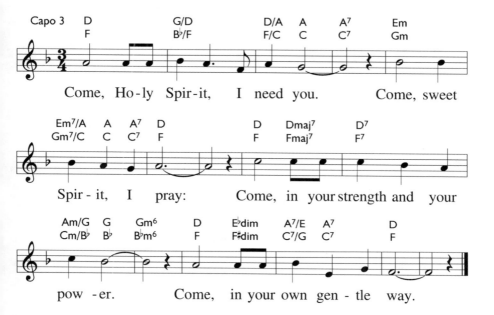

Come, Ho-ly Spir-it, I need you. Come, sweet
Spir-it, I pray: Come, in your strength and your
pow-er. Come, in your own gen-tle way.

Words: William J. & Gloria Gaither
Music: William J. Gaither
Words and music copyright © 1964 William J. Gaither, Inc.
All rights controlled by Gaither Copyright Management. Used by permission.

Come, Holy Spirit

111

Come, Ho-ly Spir-it, gra-cious heaven-ly
dove; come, fire of love.

Words: traditional
Music: The Iona Community 1988
Music copyright © 1988 by WGRG The Iona Community (Scotland). Used by permission of GIA Publications, Inc.

Come into God's Presence

Come in - to God's pres - ence sing - ing, "Al- le - lu - ia,

al - le - lu - ia, al - le - lu - ia."

Additional verses:

Come into God's presence singing, "Joy to the world."
"Songs that will heal."
"Hope for the earth."
"Love is the way."
"Glory to God."

Words: traditional   *Music:* traditional

113

O-so-so

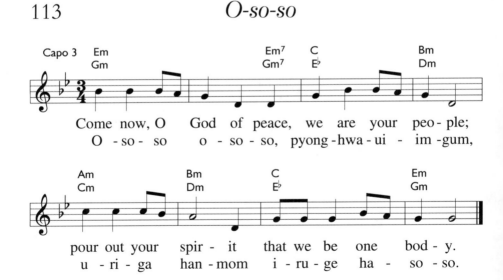

Come now, O   God   of peace,   we   are   your   peo - ple;
O - so - so   o - so - so,   pyong - hwa - ui - im - gum,

pour out your   spir - it   that we   be   one   bod - y.
u - ri - ga   han - mom   i - ru - ge   ha - so - so.

Words: Korean, Geonyong Lee, English translation Marion Pope
Music: Geonyong Lee
Words and music copyright © 1995 Geonyong Lee. Translation copyright © 1996 Marion Pope.

Daily Bread

114

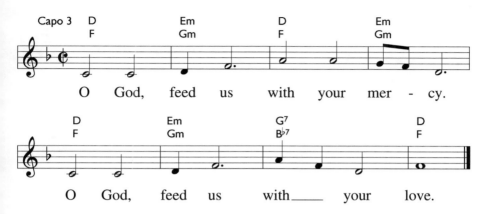

O God, feed us with your mer - cy.
O God, feed us with___ your love.

Words: Suzanne Toolan   *Music:* Suzanne Toolan
Reprinted from *Canticles and Gathering Prayers* (Mossi/Toolan, 1989), Saint Mary's Press, Winona, MN.
Used by permission of the publisher. All rights reserved.

Dear God, You Hear Us

115

Dear God, you hear us when we pray, in what we
think and what we say. With hearts of love we come to
you, and bring our prayers for oth - ers too.

Words: Flora & Wayne   *Music:* Flora & Wayne
Words and music copyright © 1994, 1998 Flora Litt & Wayne Irwin.

116   *Fill My Cup*

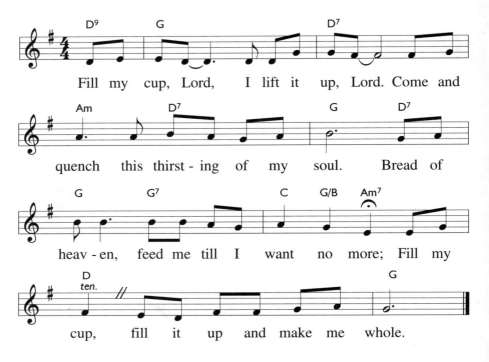

Fill my cup, Lord, I lift it up, Lord. Come and quench this thirst-ing of my soul. Bread of heav-en, feed me till I want no more; Fill my cup, fill it up and make me whole.

Words: Richard Blanchard/Sacred Songs   *Music:* Richard Blanchard/Sacred Songs

117   *Gathered in Love*

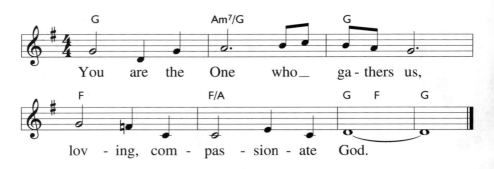

You are the One who_ ga - thers us, lov - ing, com - pas - sion - ate God.

Words: Suzanne Toolan   *Music:* Suzanne Toolan

Give Me a New Heart, O God   118

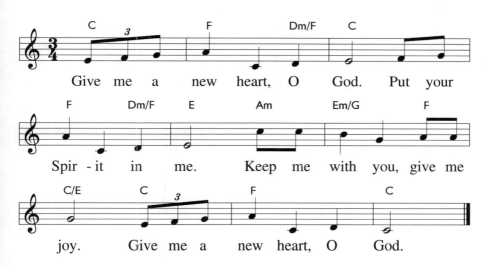

Give me a new heart, O God. Put your
Spir - it in me. Keep me with you, give me
joy. Give me a new heart, O God.

Words: Christopher Walker   *Music:* Christopher Walker

Occuli Nostri   119

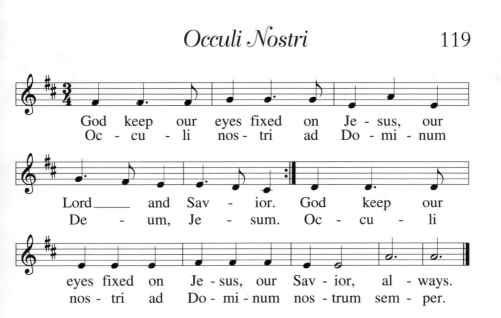

God keep our eyes fixed on Je - sus, our
Oc - cu - li nos - tri ad Do - mi - num

Lord_____ and Sav - ior. God keep our
De - um, Je - sum. Oc - cu - li

eyes fixed on Je - sus, our Sav - ior, al - ways.
nos - tri ad Do - mi - num nos - trum sem - per.

Words: traditional   *Music:* The Iona Community 1988

Hear My Words

Hear_____ my words, oh__ God, lis-ten to my
sigh-ing. Hear_____ my words, oh___
God, lis-ten to my prayers.

Words: Andrew Dreitcer
Music: Stephen Iverson
Arrangement: Michael McCarty

I Will Be Glad

Words: Psalm 9:2
Music: Daniel Charles Damon
Music copyright © 1999 by Hope Publishing Co.,
Carol Stream, IL 60188. All rights reserved. Used by permission.

In the Heart of God

In the heart of God   calm and qui - et is my soul,

As a lit - tle   child,   rest - ing   in   its
                                                            (her/his)

moth - er's   arms.   Ooh_____ (ooh)
(fath - er's)

Words: Andrew Dreitcer
Music: Stephen Iverson
Arrangement: Michael McCarty
Words copyright © 1997 Andrew Dreitcer.
Music copyright © 1997 Stephen Iverson.
Arrangement copyright © 1998 Mimesis Press.

The Jesus Prayer

123

Je - sus Christ, Son of God, have mer - cy on me.

Words: traditional
Music: Stephen Iverson
Arrangement: Michael McCarty
Music copyright © 1997 Stephen Iverson.
Arrangement copyright © 1998 Mimesis Press.

Kindle a Flame

124

Kin - dle a flame to light - en the

dark and take all fear a - way.

Words: The Iona Community 1987
Music: The Iona Community 1987
Words and music copyright © 1987 WGRG The Iona Community (Scotland).
Used by permission of GIA Publications, Inc.

125

He Is Lord

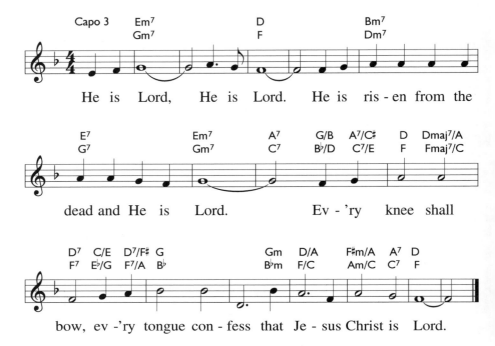

He is Lord, He is Lord. He is ris - en from the

dead and He is Lord. Ev - 'ry knee shall

bow, ev - 'ry tongue con - fess that Je - sus Christ is Lord.

Words: traditional
Music: traditional

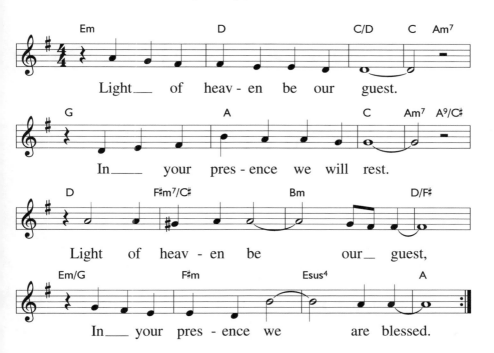

Light___ of heav - en be our guest.

In___ your pres - ence we will rest.

Light of heav - en be our___ guest,

In___ your pres - ence we are blessed.

Words: Andrew Dreitcer   *Music:* Stephen Iverson   *Arrangement:* Michael McCarty
Words copyright © 1997 Andrew Dreitcer. Music copyright © 1997 Stephen Iverson. Arrangement copyright © 1998 Mimesis Press.

Listen in the Silence 127

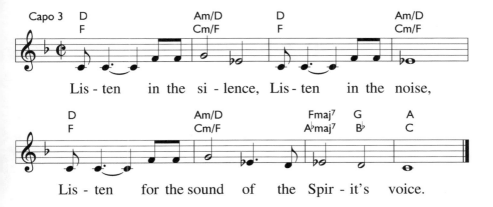

Lis - ten in the si - lence, Lis - ten in the noise,

Lis - ten for the sound of the Spir - it's voice.

Words: Linnea Good
Music: Linnea Good
Words and music copyright © 1998 Borealis Music.

Lord, I Long to Be Holy

Ho - ly, ho - ly, Lord, I long to be ho - ly.

Je - sus, Je - sus, come and make me ho - ly.

Change__ me, change__ me from glo - ry to glo - ry.

Ho - ly, ho - ly, Lord, I long to be ho - ly.

Words: Ruth Fazal
Music: Ruth Fazal
Words and music copyright © 1995 Ruth Fazal.

Lord, Listen to Your Children

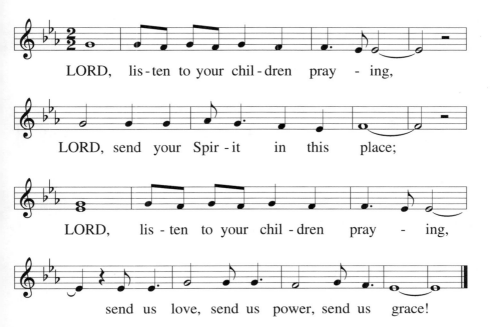

LORD, lis-ten to your chil-dren pray - ing,

LORD, send your Spir-it in this place;

LORD, lis-ten to your chil-dren pray - ing,

send us love, send us power, send us grace!

Words: Ken Medema
Music: Ken Medema
Words and music copyright © 1973 by Hope Publishing Co.,
Carol Stream, IL 60188. All rights reserved. Used by permission.

Listen to My prayer

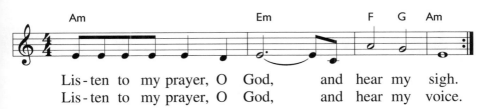

Lis-ten to my prayer, O God, and hear my sigh.
Lis-ten to my prayer, O God, and hear my voice.

Words: Psalm 3, paraphrased
Music: Handt Hanson
Words and music copyright © 1985 Changing Church, Inc.
Used with permission of Changing Church, Inc./Prince of Peace Publishing.

131

Nada Te Turbe

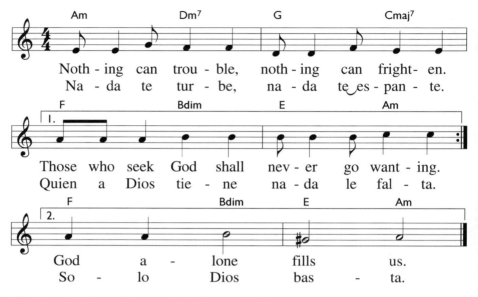

Noth - ing can trou - ble, noth - ing can fright- en.
Na - da te tur - be, na - da te es - pan - te.

1.
Those who seek God shall nev - er go want - ing.
Quien a Dios tie - ne na - da le fal - ta.

2.
God a - lone fills us.
So - lo Dios bas - ta.

Words: Spanish St. Teresa of Jesus, trans. Taizé Community 1986
Music: Jacques Berthier 1991
Words and music copyright © 1986, 1991 Les Presses de Taizé (France). Used by permission of GIA Publications, Inc.

132

O God Hear My Prayer

O God hear my prayer, O God hear my prayer:

when I call an - swer me. O God hear my prayer, O

God hear my prayer: come and lis - ten to me.

Words: Jacques Berthier, alt   *Music:* Jacques Berthier
Words and music copyright © Les Presses de Taizé (France). Used by permission of GIA Publications, Inc.

O God We Call

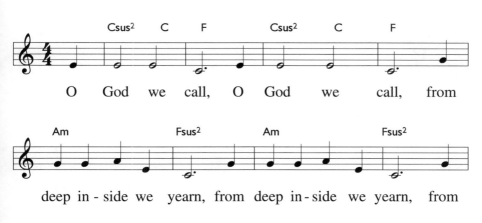

O God we call, O God we call, from

deep in - side we yearn, from deep in - side we yearn, from

deep in - side we yearn for you.

Words: Linnea Good
Music: Linnea Good
Words and music copyright © 1994 Borealis Music.

Peace Be Still

Peace be still peace___ be still the

storm___ ra - ges peace, be still.

Words: Stephen Iverson
Music: Stephen Iverson
Arrangement: Michael McCarty
Words and music copyright © 1997 Stephen Iverson. Arrangement copyright © 1998 Mimesis Press.

135
Open Our Hearts

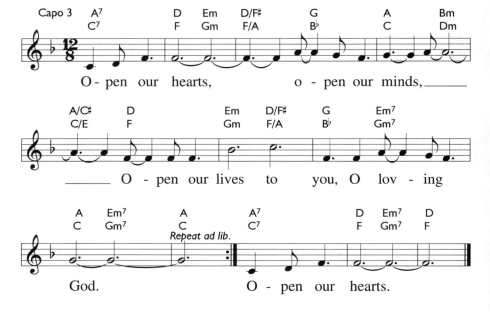

O - pen our hearts, o - pen our minds, _____ _____ O - pen our lives to you, O lov - ing God. O - pen our hearts.

Words: Jim Strathdee *Music:* Jim Strathdee
Words and music copyright © 1997 by Desert Flower Music, Carmichael, CA.

136
Peace I Am

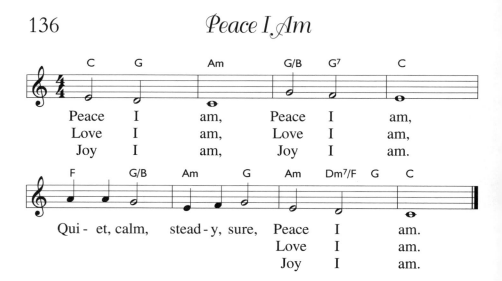

Peace I am, Peace I am,
Love I am, Love I am,
Joy I am, Joy I am.

Qui - et, calm, stead - y, sure, Peace I am.
Love I am.
Joy I am.

Words: Barbara Neighbors Deal *Music:* Barbara Neighbors Deal
Words and music copyright © 1990 AmaDeus Group.

O Great Spirit 137

Tune: O Great Spirit

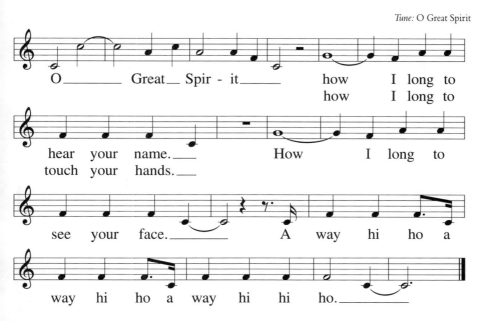

O_____ Great_ Spir - it_____ how I long to
                                   how I long to

hear your name.___ How I long to
touch your hands.___

see your face._____ A way hi ho a

way hi ho a way hi hi ho._____

Words: Doreen Clellamin 1993, adapt. 1994
Music: Doreen Clellamin
Words and music adapted from a song by Nuxalk Young People. Words and music copyright © 1994 Doreen Clellamin.

Send Your Holy Spirit 138

Tune: Joyner

Send your Ho - ly Spir-it, send your Ho - ly Spir-it,
Alt. words Send your Ho - ly Spir-it on your gath - ered peo-ple,

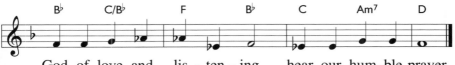

God of love and lis - ten - ing, hear our hum-ble prayer.
mer - ci - ful and lov - ing God, hear us, as we pray.

Words: Jim Strathdee *Music:* Jim Strathdee
Words and music copyright © 1994 by Desert Flower Music, Carmichael, CA.

139

Take Me, God

Take me, God. I give to you ev - 'ry - thing and all I do— my

love, my life is my of - fer - ing that I give to you.

Words: Handt Hanson
Music: Handt Hanson
Words and music copyright © 1985 Changing Church, Inc.
Used with permission of Changing Church, Inc./Prince of Peace Publishing.

140

Through Our Lives

Through our lives and by our prayers your King - dom come.

Words: The Iona Community
Music: The Iona Community
Words and music copyright © 1987 WGRG The Iona Community (Scotland).
Used by permission of GIA Publications, Inc.

Water Our Lives

Wa-ter our lives, with ev-er flow-ing streams

of your grace. Bear in our lives, cre-a-ting

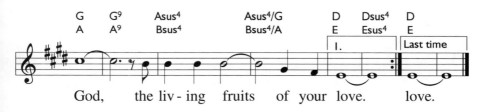

God, the liv-ing fruits of your love. love.

Words: Andrew Dreitcer
Music: Stephen Iverson
Arrangement: Michael McCarty
Words copyright © 1997 Andrew Dreitcer.
Music copyright © 1997 Stephen Iverson.
Arrangement copyright © 1998 Mimesis Press.

142 *Ways of Wisdom*

Let us fol - low ways of Wis - dom and de -
light in ways of Wis - dom. All her paths __ are
peace. __ All her paths ___ are peace. ___
All her paths __ are peace. Let us peace.

Words: Andrew Dreitcer   *Music:* Andrew Dreitcer
Arrangement: Michael McCarty
Words and music copyright © 1997 Andrew Dreitcer. Arrangement copyright © 1998 Mimesis Press.

143 *Word of Christ*

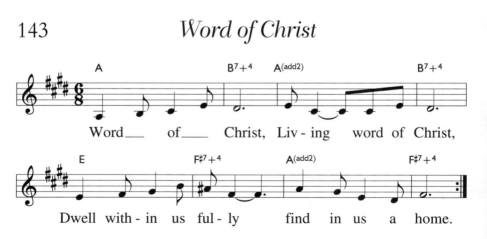

Word __ of __ Christ, Liv - ing word of Christ,
Dwell with - in us ful - ly find in us a home.

Words: Andrew Dreitcer   *Music:* Stephen Iverson
Arrangement: Michael McCarty
Words copyright © 1997 Andrew Dreitcer. Music copyright © 1997 Stephen Iverson. Arrangement copyright © 1998 Mimesis Press.

You Will Seek Me and Find Me 144

Tune: Barrett

You will seek me and find me, when you search for me with all your heart. You will seek me and find me, when you search for me with all your heart.

Words: Daniel Charles Damon
Music: Daniel Charles Damon

Deep Waters 145

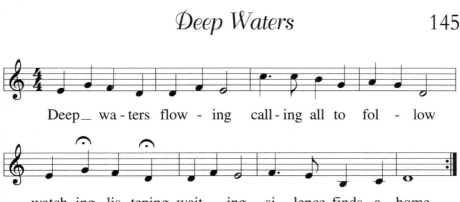

Deep_ wa-ters flow - ing call-ing all to fol - low watch -ing, lis -tening, wait - ing si - lence finds a home.

Words: Trisha Watts
Music: Trisha Watts

146   *Heal Me*

I__ will live for you a - lone, for you a - lone I'll

live. Heal me, heal me, heal me and let me__ live.

Words: Trisha Watts
Music: Trisha Watts
Words and music copyright © 1992 Trisha Watts, Willow Connection Pty Ltd., Sydney.

147   *Icon of Grace*

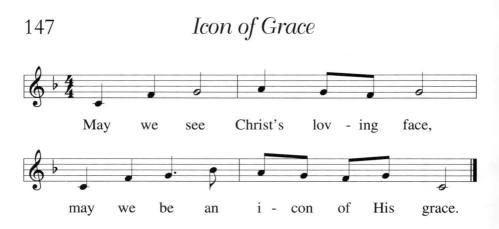

May   we   see   Christ's   lov - ing   face,

may   we   be   an   i - con   of   His   grace.

Words: Trisha Watts
Music: Trisha Watts
Words and music copyright © 1992 Trisha Watts, Willow Connection Pty Ltd., Sydney.

Justice Cry

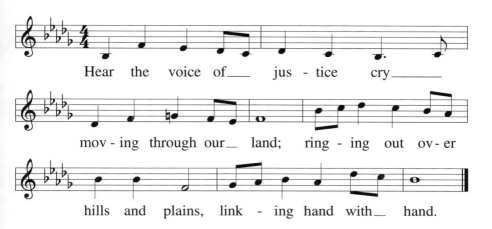

Hear the voice of__ jus - tice cry_____
mov - ing through our__ land; ring - ing out ov - er
hills and plains, link - ing hand with__ hand.

Words: Trisha Watts   *Music:* Trisha Watts
Words and music copyright © 1992 Trisha Watts, Willow Connection Pty Ltd., Sydney.

Like a Tree

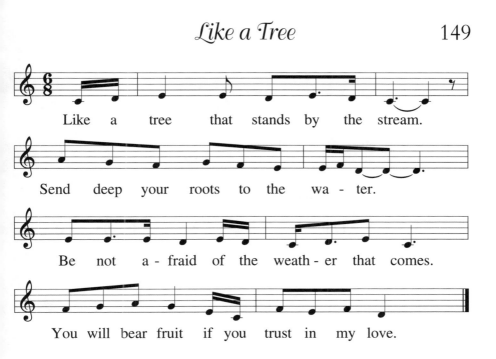

Like a tree that stands by the stream.
Send deep your roots to the wa - ter.
Be not a - fraid of the weath - er that comes.
You will bear fruit if you trust in my love.

Words: Trisha Watts   *Music:* Trisha Watts
Words and music copyright © 1992 Trisha Watts, Willow Connection Pty Ltd., Sydney.

150 **Rest and Wait**

Rest and wait in the wild - er - ness
lis - ten and see with your heart. Come!__

Words: Trisha Watts
Music: Trisha Watts
Copyright © 1992 Trisha Watts, Willow Connection Pty Ltd., Sydney.

151 **Spring of Water**

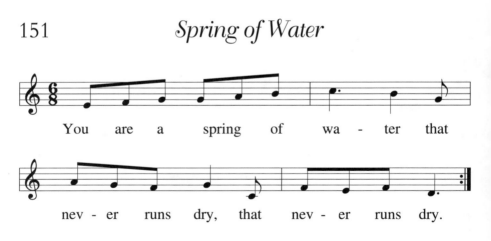

You are a spring of wa - ter that
nev - er runs dry, that nev - er runs dry.

Words: Trisha Watts
Music: Trisha Watts
Words and music copyright © 1992 Trisha Watts, Willow Connection Pty Ltd., Sydney.

Alleluia

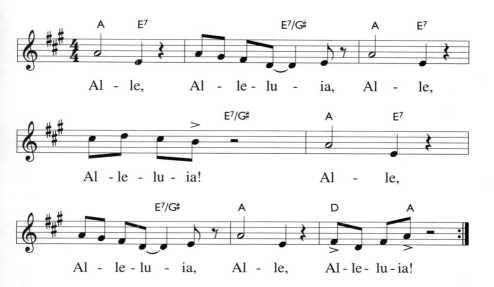

Al - le,   Al - le - lu - ia,   Al - le,

Al - le - lu - ia!   Al - le,

Al - le - lu - ia,   Al - le,   Al - le - lu - ia!

Words: traditional
Music: Michael McCarty
Music copyright © 1997 Mimesis Press

Heleluyan (Alleluia)

He - le - lu - yan, he - le - lu - yan; he - le, he - le - lu - yan;

he - le - lu - yan, he - le - lu - yan; he - le, he - le - lu - yan.

Words: traditional Muscogee Indian
Music: traditional Muscogee
Transcription: Charles H. Webb

Give Ear, O People/God Has Spoken

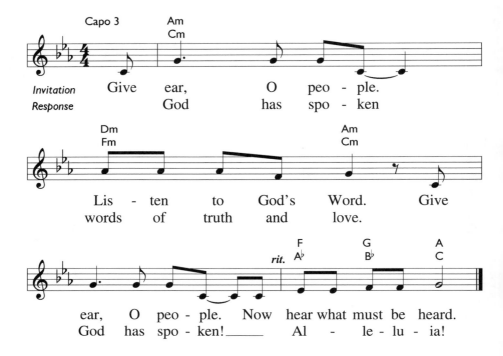

Invitation Give ear, O peo - ple.
Response God has spo - ken

Lis - ten to God's Word. Give
words of truth and love.

ear, O peo - ple. Now hear what must be heard.
God has spo - ken!_____ Al - le - lu - ia!

Words: Darrell Faires, Sr.
Music: Darrell Faires, Sr.
From *Singable Liturgy.* Words and music copyright © 1997 by Shalom Publications, Hazelwood, MO.
Used by permission.

155   *Amen (Great)*

A - men, a - men, a - men.

Words: traditional
Music: Kevin Mayhew
Music copyright © Kevin Mayhew Ltd. Buxhall, Stowmark, Suffolk.
Used by permission.

In God we live and move, In God we have our be - ing, In

God we shall re - main, In God is our a - bid - ing.

Words: Joyce Rupp, author of *Praying Our Goodbyes* and other books.
Music: Linnea Good
Words copyright Joyce Rupp.
Music copyright © 1994 Borealis Music.

157

Benediction

Capo 3

As we leave this place of wor-ship, And we
go our sep-arate ways, May the God who goes be-
fore us, Guide in all our com-ing days. Let us
now go forth in ser-vice, Serv-ing ev-'ry creed and
race; In the spir - it of true
giv - ing, Liv - ing peace and grace.

Words: William B. Petricko
Music: William B. Petricko
Words and music copyright © 1997 William B. Petricko.

The Blessing of God

Capo 3

The bless-ing of God is up - on us, and ne - ver will be ta - ken from us; we go from this place, made strong by God's grace, to live in the peace of Christ Je - sus. A - men! A - men! A - men!

Words: Flora & Wayne
Music: Flora & Wayne
Words and music copyright © 1995, 1998 Flora Litt & Wayne Irwin.

159

Go and Tell the World

Tune: Go and Tell

Go and tell the world how Je - sus lived and died.

Go and show the love of Christ, the cru - ci - fied.

Man - y have not heard the lib - er - a - ting word, then

go, and tell, and show how God is glo - ri - fied.

Words: Brian Wren
Music: Daniel Charles Damon
Words and music copyright © 1999 by Hope Publishing Co.,
Carol Stream, IL 60188. All rights reserved. Used by permission.

God Bless and Keep You

God bless and keep you, God shine up - on you,

God's grac - ious pre - sence a - bide with you in peace.

God bless and keep you, God shine up - on you,

God's grac - ious pre - sence a - bide with you in peace.

Words: Andrew Dreitcer
Music: Judy Hunnicutt, from the anthem May the Lord Bless You
Words copyright © 1998 Andrew Dreitcer.
Music copyright © 1985 The Sacred Music Press, Div. of Lorenz Corporation.

Send Us Out

Send us out in the pow - er of Your Spir - it LORD.

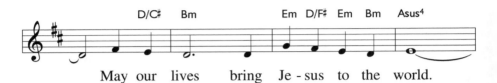

May our lives bring Je - sus to the world.

May each thought and word bring glo - ry to Your name;

Send us out in Your Spir - it LORD we pray.

Words: Ruth Fazal
Music: Ruth Fazal
Words and music copyright © 1993 Ruth Fazal. All rights reserved. International copyright secured.

162

Kyrie

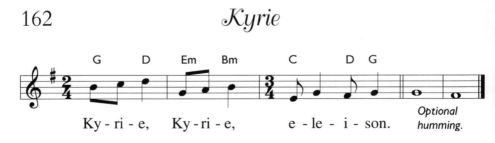

Ky - ri - e, Ky - ri - e, e - le - i - son.

Optional humming.

Words: traditional
Music: Jacques Berthier
Music copyright © 1981 Les Presses de Taizé (France). Used by permission of GIA Publications, Inc.

Kyrie

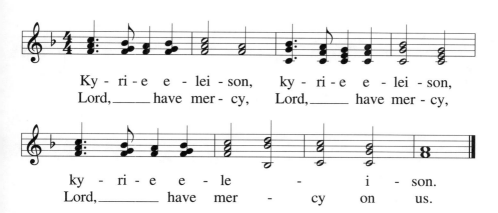

Ky - ri - e e - lei - son, ky - ri - e e - lei - son,
Lord,_____ have mer - cy, Lord,_____ have mer - cy,

ky - ri - e e - le - i - son.
Lord,_____ have mer - cy on us.

Words: traditional
Music: Russian Orthodox liturgy

Kyrie Eleison

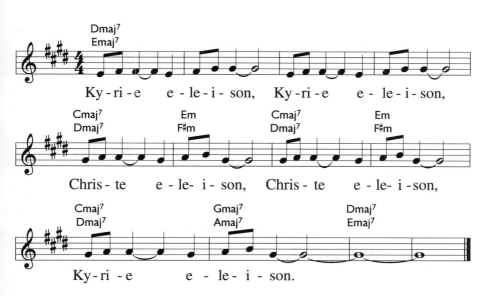

Ky - ri - e e - le - i - son, Ky - ri - e e - le - i - son,

Chris - te e - le - i - son, Chris - te e - le - i - son,

Ky - ri - e e - le - i - son.

Words: traditional
Music: Linnea Good
Copyright © 1995 Borealis Music.

Memorial Acclamation

Christ has died, Christ is ris-en, Christ will come a - gain! gain!

Words: from an ancient liturgy for the Lord's Supper
Music: James A. Kriewald
Music copyright © 1985 The United Methodist Publishing House. (Administered by The Copyright Company, Nashville, TN.)

166 *Sanctus*

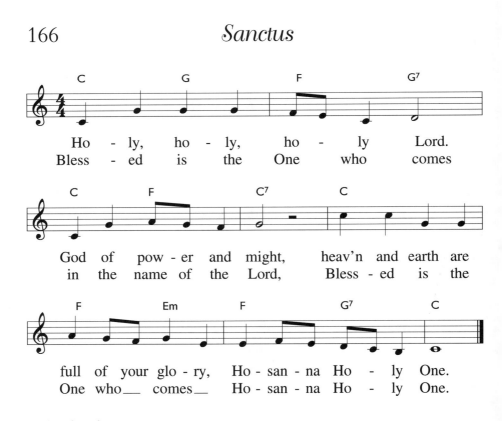

Ho - ly, ho - ly, ho - ly Lord.
Bless - ed is the One who comes

God of pow - er and might, heav'n and earth are
in the name of the Lord, Bless - ed is the

full of your glo - ry, Ho - san - na Ho - ly One.
One who__ comes__ Ho - san - na Ho - ly One.

Words: traditional
Music: Nancy Chegus
Copyright © 1992 Nancy Chegus.

Holy, Holy, Holy, God of Power and Might   167

Tune: Crestwood

Ho-ly, ho-ly, ho - ly, God of power and might;

heav - en and earth are full of your glo - ry: Ho -

san - na in the high - est! Bless - ed is the One   who

comes in the name of God: Ho-san - na in the high - est!

Words: Daniel Charles Damon
Music: Daniel Charles Damon

168   *Litany for the Breaking of the Bread*

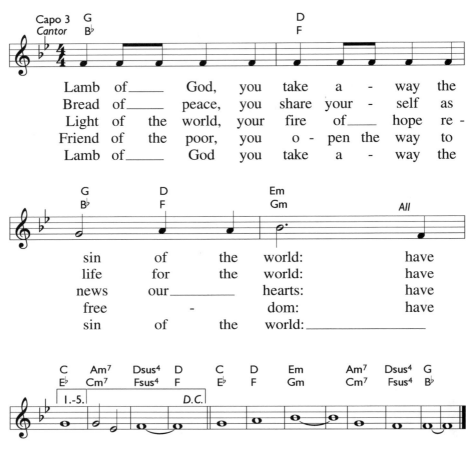

Lamb of____ God, you take a - way the
Bread of____ peace, you share your - self as
Light of the world, your fire of____ hope re -
Friend of the poor, you o - pen the way to
Lamb of____ God you take a - way the

sin of the world: have
life for the world: have
news our____ hearts: have
free - dom: have
sin of the world:____ have

Vs. 1-4 mer - cy on us.

Vs.5 grant us__ peace! Grant us peace! Grant us peace!

Words: Weston Priory & Mary David Callahan
Music: Weston Priory & Mary David Callahan
Copyright 1993, 1994, from the recording *Formed From This Earth*,
The Benedictine Foundation of the State of Vermont, Inc. Weston Priory, Weston, Vermont, USA.
This arrangement by the Monks of Weston Priory and Sister Mary David Callahan, OSB.

Mass for All Saints

a. Lord, Have Mercy

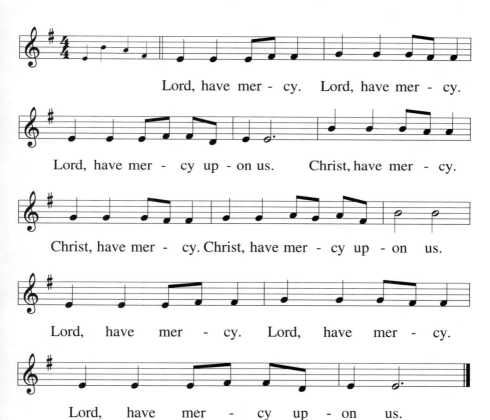

Lord, have mer - cy. Lord, have mer - cy.

Lord, have mer - cy up - on us. Christ, have mer - cy.

Christ, have mer - cy. Christ, have mer - cy up - on us.

Lord, have mer - cy. Lord, have mer - cy.

Lord, have mer - cy up - on us.

Words: traditional
Music: Mimi Farra
Copyright © 1981 Celebration.
(Administered by The Copyright Company, Nashville, TN.)
All rights reserved. International copyright secured. Used by permission.

b. Holy, Holy

Holy, ho - ly, ho - ly Lord,___

God of pow - er, God of___ pow'r and might,

heav'n and earth are full of your glo - ry. Ho - san - na,

ho - san - na, ho - san - na in the high - est.

Bless - ed is he who comes in the name of the Lord.

Ho - san - na, ho - san - na,

ho - san - na in the high - est.

Words: traditional
Music: Mimi Farra
Copyright © 1981 Celebration.
(Administered by The Copyright Company, Nashville, TN.)
All rights reserved. International copyright secured. Used by permission.

c. Our Father

With strength

Our_ Fa-ther in_ hea-ven, hal-lowed be_ your_ name. your_ king-dom come your_ will be done on_ earth_ as in hea-ven. Give us to-day_ our dai-ly bread._____ For-give us our sins as we for-give those who sin a-gainst us. Save us from the time of tri-al, and de-liv-er us_from e-vil. For the king-dom, the pow-er, and the glo-ry are yours, now and for ev-er. A-men.

Words: traditional
Music: Betty Carr Pulkingham
Arrangement: Mimi Farra
Copyright © 1981 Celebration. (Administered by The Copyright Company, Nashville, TN.)
All rights reserved. International copyright secured. Used by permission.

d. Lamb of God

With strength

Lamb___ of God, you take a-way the sins of the world;___ have mer-cy up-on us.

Lamb__ of God,__ you take a-way the sins of the world; have mer-cy up-on us. Lamb__ of God, you take a-way the sins of the world;___ grant__ us peace._____

Words: traditional
Music: Mimi Farra
Copyright © 1981 Celebration.
(Administered by The Copyright Company, Nashville, TN.)

a. Lord Have Mercy

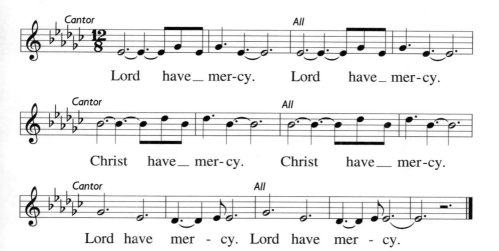

Lord have mer-cy. Lord have mer-cy.

Christ have mer-cy. Christ have mer-cy.

Lord have mer - cy. Lord have mer - cy.

Words: traditional
Music: Stephen M. Lee

b. Gloria

Words: traditional
Music: Stephen M. Lee
Copyright © 1997 Professional Music Services, Inc., New Orleans, LA.
All rights reserved. Used by permission.

c. Memorial Acclamation

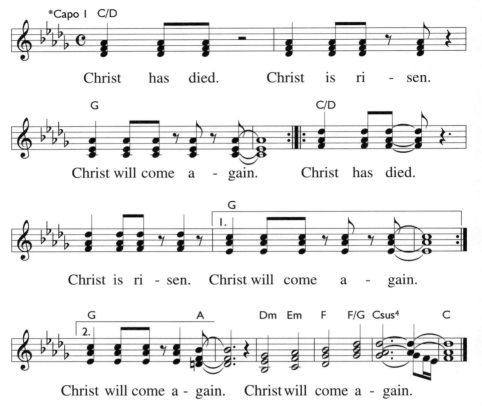

Christ has died. Christ is ri - sen. Christ will come a - gain. Christ has died. Christ is ri - sen. Christ will come a - gain. Christ will come a - gain. Christ will come a - gain.

*The chords are for the use of guitarists only.

Words: traditional
Music: Stephen M. Lee
Copyright © 1997 Professional Music Services, Inc., New Orleans, LA.
All rights reserved. Used by permission.

d. Holy, Holy

Ho - ly, ho - ly, ho - ly Lord, God of power and might. Hea -ven and_ earth are filled_ with your glo - ry. Ho - san - na in_ the_ high - est. Bless - ed is He who comes_ in the name_____ of the Lord, of the Lord. Ho - san - na in_the_ high - est, Ho - san - na in_ the_ high - est.

*The chords are for the use of guitarists only.

Words: traditional
Music: Stephen M. Lee

e. *Lamb of God*

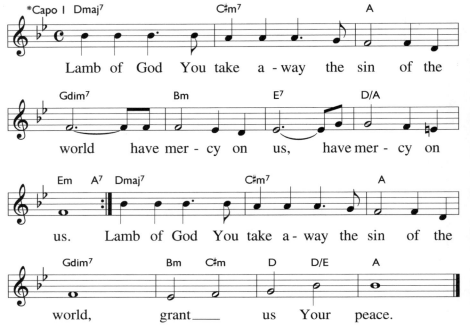

Lamb of God You take a - way the sin of the world have mer - cy on us, have mer - cy on us. Lamb of God You take a - way the sin of the world, grant___ us Your peace.

*The chords are for the use of guitarists only.

Words: traditional
Music: Stephen M. Lee
Copyright © 1997 Professional Music Services, Inc., New Orleans, LA.
All rights reserved. Used by permission.

a. Kyrie

Ky- ri - e e - le - i -son. Ky - ri - e e - le - i -son.

Ky- ri- e e - le- i -son. Chris- te e - le - i - son.

Chris - te e - le - i - son. Chris -te e - le - i - son.

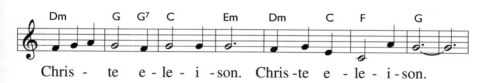

Ky - ri - e e - le - i - son. Ky - ri - e e -

le - i - son. Ky - ri - e e - le - i - son.

Words: traditional
Music: Gordon Light
Copyright © St. George's Anglican Church, Edmonton, AB.

b. Gloria

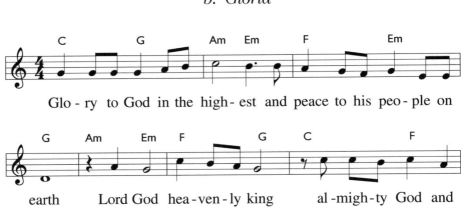

Glo - ry to God in the high- est and peace to his peo - ple on

earth   Lord God hea - ven - ly king   al - migh-ty God and

Fa - ther.   We wor-ship you, we___ give you thanks,

we praise you for your glo - ry. Lord Je - sus Christ, on- ly

Son   of the Fa - ther.   Lord   God, Lamb of God.

You take a - way the__ sins of the world,   have mer - cy on

us.   You are seat - ed on the right hand of the Fa -ther,

re - ceive our__ prayer.   For you a - lone are the

ho - ly one;   you a -lone are the Lord.   You a - lone

are   the most   high,   Je - sus   Christ with   the

Ho - ly Spir - it in the glo -ry of God the Fa -ther. A - men.

Words: traditional
Music: Gordon Light
Copyright © St. George's Anglican Church, Edmonton, AB.

c. Sanctus

Ho-ly, ho-ly, ho-ly Lord. God of power and might.

Heav'n and earth are full of your glo-ry, Ho-san-na in the

high-est. Bless-ed is He who comes in the name of the

Lord. Ho-san-na, ho-san-na, ho-san-na in the high-est.

Words: traditional
Music: Gordon Light
Copyright © St. George's Anglican Church, Edmonton, AB.

d. Lord's Prayer

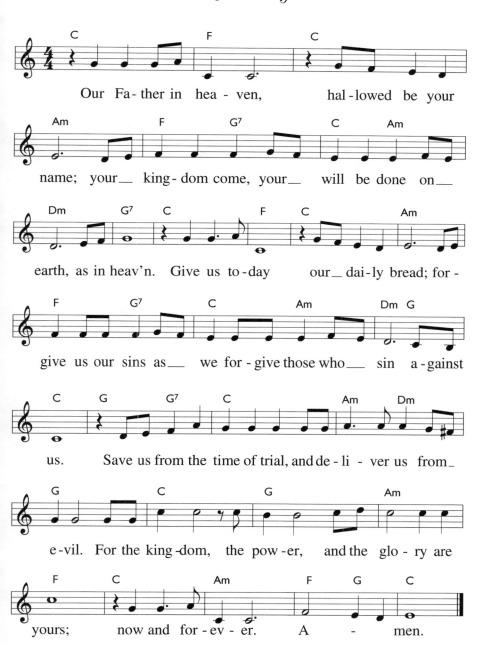

Our Fa-ther in hea-ven, hal-lowed be your name; your__ king-dom come, your__ will be done on__ earth, as in heav'n. Give us to-day our__ dai-ly bread; for-give us our sins as__ we for-give those who__ sin a-gainst us. Save us from the time of trial, and de-li-ver us from_ e-vil. For the king-dom, the pow-er, and the glo-ry are yours; now and for-ev-er. A - men.

Words: traditional
Music: Gordon Light
Copyright © St. George's Anglican Church, Edmonton, AB.

e. Agnus Dei

Lamb of God, You take a - way the sin of the world, have mer - cy on us. Lamb of God,

You take a - way the sin of the world, have mer - cy on us. Lamb of God, You take a -

way the sin of the world.____ Grant us your peace.

Words: traditional
Music: Gordon Light
Copyright © St. George's Anglican Church, Edmonton, AB.

Copyright Holder Information

Abramsky, David
814 Watson Road S
Arkell, ON N0B 1C0

AmaDeus Group
15 – 410 Church Road
Ojai, CA 93023

Benedictine Foundation of
the State of Vermont, Inc.,
The Weston Priory
Productions
58 Priory Hill Road
Weston, VT 05161

Borealis Music
311 – 1424 Walnut Street
Vancouver, BC V6J 3R3

Brentwood-Benson Music
Publishing, Inc.
365 Great Circle Road
Nashville, TN 37228-1799

Changing Church, Inc.
200 East Nicollet Boulevard
Burnsville, MN 55337

Chegus, Nancy
4 Oriole Court
St. Albert, AB T8N 6L7

Clellamin, Doreen
Box 498
Bella Coola, BC V0T 1C0

Cleveland, Paul Jefferson
2119 E 96th Street, #2
Chicago, IL 60617

Common Cup Company
7591 Gray Avenue
Burnaby, BC V5J 3Z4

Copyright Company, The
40 Music Square East
Nashville, TN 37203

Crow, Rosemary
33 Deerhaven Lane
Asheville, NC 228803

Desert Flower Music
PO Box 1476
Carmichael, CA 95609

Dreicter, Andrew
2 Kensington Road
San Anselmo, CA
94960-2905

EMI Christian Music
Publishing
PO Box 5085
Brentwood, TN 37024

Fazal, Ruth
296 Glebemount Avenue
Toronto, ON M4C 3V3

Gaither Copyright
Management
PO Box 737
Alexandria, IN 46001

GIA Publications, Inc.
7404 S. Mason Avenue
Chicago, IL 60638

Hamblen Music
c/o Cohen and Cohen
740 North La Brea Avenue,
Second Floor
Los Angeles, CA
90038-3339

Hope Publishing Co.
380 South Main Place
Carol Stream, IL 60188

Integrity Music, Inc.
c/o Integrity Incorporated
1000 Cody Road
Mobile, AL 36695

Iverson, Stephen
PO Box 1166
Fairfax, CA 94978

K & R Music, Inc.
PO Box 623
Churchville, MD 21028

Kai, David
1022 Arrowhead Place
Orleans, ON K1C 2S4

Kevin Mayhew Ltd.
Buxhall, Stowmarket,
Suffolk, IP14 3DJ U.K.

Lankshear-Smith, Doreen
PO Box 3791
Thunder Bay, ON P7B 6E3

Lee, Geonyong
Korean National
Institute of Arts
700 Seocho-dong
Deocho-gu
Seoul, Koria

Lee, Stephen M.
see Professional Music
Services, Inc.

Litt, Flora & Irwin, Wayne
11 Pirie Drive, Unit 41
Dundas, ON L9H 6Z6

Lorenz Corporation, The
PO Box 802
Dayton, OH 45401-0802

Lynch, David
599 West End Avenue,
Apt 7B
New York, NY 10024

McDade, Carolyn
PO Box 510
Wellfleet, MA 02667

Mercy/Vineyard Publishing
Music Services
209 Chapelwood Drive
Franklin, TN 37069

Mimesis Press
38 Wreden
Fairfax, CA 94930

Copyright Holder Information (cont'd)

MorningStar Music
Publishers
2117 59th Street
St. Louis, MO 63118

New Dawn Music
see OCP Publications

North American Liturgy
Resources (NALR)
see OCP Publications

OCP Publications
5536 NE Hassalo
Portland, OR 97213

Petricko, William
4031-B 4th Street
Whitehorse, YT
Y1A 1G8

Pinson, Joe
2320 Salado
Denton, TX 76201

Pope, Marion
Apt. 135, 211 College Street
Toronto, ON M5T 1R1

Prairie Rose Publications
1050 North Arnason Street
Regina, SK S4X 4K9

Professional Music
Services, Inc.
PO Box 791444
New Orleans, LA

70179-1444
Rupp, Joyce
2816 Shady Oak Drive
Des Moinse, IA 50310

Saint Mary's Press
702 Terrace Heights
Winona, MN 55987-1320

Sam, Jeeva
154 Sangster Boulevard
Regina, SK S4R 6L5

Selah Publishing Company
58 Pearl Street
PO Box 3037
Kingston, NY 12401-0902

Shalom Publications
7225 Berkridge
Hazelwood, MO 63042

Sovereign Music UK
PO Box 356
Leighton Buzzard, Beds
LU7 8WP U.K.

St. George's Anglican
Church
11733 - 87th Avenue
Edmonton, AB T6G 0Y4

Stainer & Bell Ltd
see Hope Publishing Co.

Swanson, Sue
1258 Saddlebrook Lane
Saint Paul, MN 55125

Unitarian Universalist
Association
25 Beacon Street
Boston, MA 02108

Walker, Jack
Brentwood Presbyterian
Church
12000 San Vicente Boulevard
Los Angeles, CA 90049

Walton Music Corporation
170 NE 33rd Street
Ft. Lauderdale, FL 33334

Willow Connection Pty Ltd.
7A, 3-9 Kenneth Road
Manly Vale, NSW, 2093
Australia

Word Music, Inc.
PO Box 128469
Nashville, TN 37212-8469

Index

Note: song titles are printed in italics

Other Music Resources
Available from Wood Lake Books

Songs for A Gospel People
This popular songbook reflects a worldwide, ecumenical heritage.
Inclusive language. Paperback with coil binding.
Available in large print edition.

Spirit of Singing
A collection of songs that you might have learned around the campfire.
From a variety of traditions. Paperback with coil binding.

All God's Children Sing
A broad selection of music for children and intergenerational singing.
Paperback with coil binding. Also available on cassette.

Hymns We Love to Sing – Large Print
Old and new favorites in an easier-to-see format.
Words and music edition, and words only hymnal.
Paperback with coil binding.

Music for Wedding Services
A collection of music, hymns, Psalm settings, and solos.
Couple's planner, musician's book, congregational booklet,
and cassette available.

Wood Lake Books also has music by Jean & Jim Strathdee,
Jim Manley, Lesley Clare, and Paul Crowder.